Concept, editing, production
GörmanGruppen AB, Malmö.
 Lill Forsman, Camilla Görman, Curt
 Görman, Björn Halling, Gun Larsson,
 Bengt Pernfors, Bosse Persson.
 Translation: Roger Tanner.

Food and drink co-ordination
Björn Halling, Principal,
Restaurangakademien, Stockholm
Robert Bergquist, Product Adviser,
Systembolaget, Malmö.

Recipe checking
Berit Selén, Home Economics Teacher,
Eskilstuna.

Feature articles
A. Stellan Karlsson, Christina Mattsson,
Bosse Persson, Anders Salomonsson,
Jan-Öjvind Swahn.

Drawings
Carl Larsson, Nationalmuseum, pp. 54-55.
Einar Nerman/BUS 1994, p. 83.
Jean Eric Rehn, p. 15.
Johan Tobias Sergel, s. 17.
Anders Zorn, s. 9.
Other drawings: Curt Görman.

Photography, unless otherwise indicated
Gunnar Magnusson, GörmanGruppen.

Other photo credits, in page order
Bildarkivet, Hans Nelsäter AB, Stockholm,
 p. 13.
Mats Landin, Nordiska Museet, Stockholm;
 p. 16, p. 31, schnapps glass, p. 34, and table
 decoration, p. 35.
Lars Westrup, Kulturen, Lund, s. 18, p. 49
 and drinking vessel, p. 73.
Britt Olstrup, Stockholms Stadsmuseum,
 mug, p. 19.
Lars Strandberg, Malmö, p. 22-23.
Ulf Westerman, Tiofoto, Stockholm, p. 26.
Frantisek Chmura, Tiofoto, Stockholm, p. 27.
Bo Nystrand, Booster Media, Malmö, p. 28.
Anders Salomonsson, Lund, pp. 50-51.
"The New Orleans Cookbook", p. 135.

Kitchen/studio
GörmanGruppen, Malmö

Typeface
ITC Garamond

Repro/origination
Offset-Kopio, Finland

Paper
150 g. glazed Silverblade

Printing
Fälths Tryckeri, Värnamo 1994

Copyright
© 1994 GörmanGruppen/Rabén Prisma

ISBN 91-518-2804-9

The editors acknowledge
valuable assistance from

Arla Ost, Stockholm

AssiDomän, Stockholm

*Albert Engström Sällskapet,
Grisslehamn*

Ikea of Sweden AB, Älmhult

*Kronofiske Harasjömåla,
Olofström*

Kulturen, Lund

Kungliga Biblioteket, Stockholm

Nationalmuseum, Stockholm

Nordiska museet, Stockholm

Orrefors Sweden, Orrefors

*AB Ramlösa Hälsobrunn,
Helsingborg*

Riksarkivet, Stockholm

*Simontorp Aquaculture AB,
Blentarp*

*Stockholms Stadsmuseum,
Stockholm*

*Svenska Porträttarkivet, Statens
Konstmuseer, Stockholm*

Systembolaget, Stockholm

Universitetsbiblioteket, Lund

*Vin- & Sprithistoriska Museet,
Stockholm*

and

*all the relatives, colleagues
and other friends who have
gladly shared with us
their experiences of a lifetime's
crayfish guzzling.*

Crayfish Rhapsody

A culinary and historical voyage to the world of crayfish

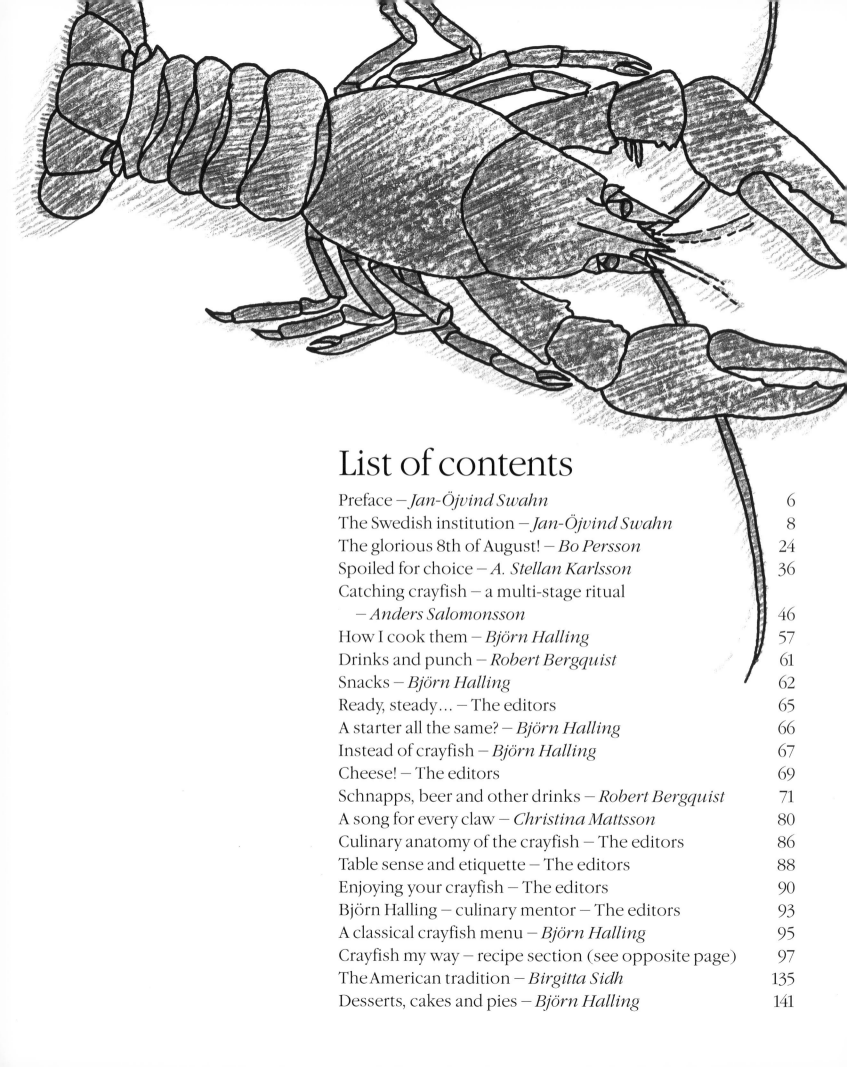

List of contents

Preface – *Jan-Öjvind Swahn* 6

The Swedish institution – *Jan-Öjvind Swahn* 8

The glorious 8th of August! – *Bo Persson* 24

Spoiled for choice – *A. Stellan Karlsson* 36

Catching crayfish – a multi-stage ritual
    – *Anders Salomonsson* 46

How I cook them – *Björn Halling* 57

Drinks and punch – *Robert Bergquist* 61

Snacks – *Björn Halling* 62

Ready, steady… – The editors 65

A starter all the same? – *Björn Halling* 66

Instead of crayfish – *Björn Halling* 67

Cheese! – The editors 69

Schnapps, beer and other drinks – *Robert Bergquist* 71

A song for every claw – *Christina Mattsson* 80

Culinary anatomy of the crayfish – The editors 86

Table sense and etiquette – The editors 88

Enjoying your crayfish – The editors 90

Björn Halling – culinary mentor – The editors 93

A classical crayfish menu – *Björn Halling* 95

Crayfish my way – recipe section (see opposite page) 97

The American tradition – *Birgitta Sidh* 135

Desserts, cakes and pies – *Björn Halling* 141

Recipe section

Old-fashioned crayfish bisque with pike mousse – *Björn Halling*   97

Crayfish salad from East Småland – *Björn Halling*   99

Nils-Emil's crayfish pâté with trout roe – *Nils-Emil Ahlin*   101

On the morrow – *Jan Boris-Möller*   102

Crayfish cocktails – *Karin Chädström*   105

Browned crayfish tails with curry sauce – *Anders Dahlbom*   107

A stew of crayfish and light-salted perch – *Thomas Dreijing*   109

Aubergine galette with crayfish – *Karin Fransson*   110

Crayfish and chanterelles in aspic – *Stefan Holmström*   112

Brochette of crayfish and shallots – *Kenneth Ingelsson*   115

Boiled crayfish in saffron broth – *Örjan Klein*   117

Stewed crayfish tails – *Gert Klötzke*   118

A "pastry" of crayfish and veal sweetbreads – *Erik Lallerstedt*   121

Crayfish mousseline on leaves of spinach – *Eric Lips*   122

Crayfish with ginger dressing and chives – *Leif Mannerström*   125

Crayfish and basil omelette – *Rickard Nilsson*   126

Blanquette, Swedish style – *Claes Riddarström*   129

A crayfish salad for August – *Severin Sjöstedt*   131

Freshwater crayfish and pike mousse – *Bengt Wedholm*   133

Crawfish fiesta – *Jonas Borssén*   135

Crawfish Cardinale – *Birgitta Sidh*   137

Crawfish Gumbo – *Jonas Borssén*   139

The oven temperatures, weights and volumes in the recipes are, respectively, in °C, kg and litres or parts thereof. Here are some basic conversion tables.

Conversion tables

Oven temperatures

°C	°F
100-150	212-300
175-225	350-425
250	475
275	525

Weights

1g	0.035 oz
10g	1/3 oz
25g	1 oz
50g	1.75 oz
100g	3.5 oz
150g	5 oz
200g	7 oz
250g	9 oz
450g	1 lb
900g	2 lb

Volumes

1 dl	3.5 fl oz
1 l	2.1 pints (US)
	1.75 pints (GB)

Preface

"The tables are decked in the orchard bower,
The lanterns are glowing, the evening is warm.
The dill weed's a-whisper,
resplendent in bloom,
And crayfish, roe-packed,
lie waiting, piled high."

This is how Erik Axel Karlfeldt, that most Swedish of Swedish poets, once described one of the most Swedish sides of Swedish living, namely a crayfish party in the soft August moonlight. Now the crayfish party is entirely a Swedish invention. Otherwise, most of our festive habits – from dancing around the Maypole to Easter eggs, Father Christmas or the Christmas tree – have been imported from the continent of Europe.

But the crayfish party and the near-ritual worship of this polypod sprang from our own hearts and minds, albeit not so very long ago. When the opening date for crayfish trapping – 8th August – was fixed, just over a hundred years ago, bureaucratic top-hampering merged with archipelago romanticism to produce a very special occasion. To begin with, that occasion was observed mainly by the nouveau riche merchant class, on the verandas of its cottages out in the skerries, but the practice spread through progressively wider reaches of the middle classes, eventually becoming a national institution.

This book sets out, in words and pictures, to describe what today is very much of a living tradition, one in which food and drink, songs and other accessories have entered into a covenant against the background and under the influence of our magical scenery. An account is given here of the biological, indeed the anatomical aspect, and the uninitiated will find everything they need to know and never dared to ask about the proper dissection and ingestion of crayfish.

Book learning, of course, has its limitations. Practice makes perfect – for example, as regards the connoisseur's knack of picking out the females from a mound of crayfish. This is a skill to be developed privately, for it is counted very bad manners at the crayfish table to return one to the pile on finding it, too late, to be of the male gender.

Personally I am one of those who maintain that the only conceivable starter for a crayfish party is crayfish, that the obvious main course is crayfish and that the dessert, *de rigeur*, must be crayfish. But readers not sharing this fixation will find a good many more varied menu suggestions, plus hints on varying the preparation of crayfish, contributed by some of Sweden's greatest food-masters.

All necessary attention is of course paid to the drinks side – not forgetting another indispensable accessory, the schnapps ditty – but even so, I think the time has come to dispel the regrettably widespread fallacy that crayfish must be washed down with schnapps by the bucketful – for example, one dram per tail or, perish the thought, one per claw. The gentle fragrance of the crayfish is in no way compatible with a superabundance of spirits. For my own part I treat the dram (in the form of ice-cold, unflavoured vodka), virtually as a kind of mouth water, its task being, together with the cheese on crisp bread, to reset the taste buds for a moment and prepare the pallet for the next gust of crayfish aroma. People who drink themselves silly at crayfish parties might just as well be served fish fingers after the first few minutes. Then there is the vexed issue of whether or not wine can be drunk with crayfish, but readers wishing to refine their habits in this direction will find useful hints on appropriate labels.

It is of course no mere coincidence, this book seeing the light of day just when open-season restrictions for crayfish have been abolished. It is a fairly safe bet, though, that its pages will above all be consulted and relished with the full moon of August in position, reddish-yellow and magnificent, over the horizon, whether that horizon be made up of conifer tops, rocks and skerries or the urban skyline.

Jan-Öjvind Swahn

Jan-Öjvind Swahn

The Swedish institution

Dear Mrs Lundström, put schnapps on ice and prepare a party for seven, with crayfish, eel and fresh radishes. Forget not the Burträsk cheese and the tenderest flat bread. Fill then the tankers with foaming ale, mixing two of ale with one of porter. Then we will have a banquet fit for Swedish men. I have spoken!

When he is not tied to the desk where, by now, he has written, co-authored or edited a couple of hundred books, Jan-Öjvind Swahn creates a soup. It is in the soup terrine that he finds an outlet for his culinary imagination, though by simple means: one of his favourites is a creamy soup of perch. Otherwise he has chugged along a wide variety of tracks, research in Lund (specialising in folk tales), university lecturing and tutoring there and in Göteborg and Uppsala, and also at the Åbo Academy in Turku, Finland, where he was made a professor. He started off in early years as a librarian, ending up as head of the Nordic Museum Library in Stockholm. In 1970 he joined Bra Böcker as an encyclopedist, becoming chief editor of Sweden's best-selling reference works through the ages and an assiduous contributor to the National Encyclopedia. He is also much in demand as a radio and television broadcaster.

Thus lightheartedly could August Strindberg, that sombre Titan of Swedish literature, pen his thoughts when inspired by the prospect of a crayfish party. There are several other instances showing how crayfish eating could put him in a lyrical frame of mind – such as the classical guide to crayfish eating which he included in the novel "Giftas". The main character, "Magistern", begins by spreading butter on the coarse bread, adding cheese and taking a dram before getting down to the real business:

When the crayfish, six in number, have been brought in, he examines their gender and, there being no objections to raise, proceeds to the pleasurable act. He tucks one corner of the napkin under his detachable collar, places two cheese sandwiches in readiness next to his plate and pours himself a glass of beer and a small dram. This done, he picks up the small crayfish knife and the butchery begins. He alone in Sweden knows how to eat crayfish, and when he happens on somebody else eating them he says: "You don't know how to eat crayfish." First he makes an incision round the crayfish's head, and then, putting the aperture to his mouth, he sucks at it.

"That," he says, "is the best part."
Then he detaches the thorax from the base, carves a "blood eagle*"
as he calls it, puts his teeth in the carcass and sucks deeply; after
this he drags off the narrow legs like asparagus. Next he eats a
pinch of dill, takes a swig of beer and bites at the sandwich. After
he has carefully shelled the claws and sucked out the finest chalk
tubes, he consumes the meat and goes on to the tail. After eating
three crayfish he takes a dram and cons the official appointments.
He has done this for twelve years now and will forever continue.

This short story takes place on a winter's evening and, true enough, was written in the days when crayfish were only prohibited during the spring and summer. The only thing I find exceptionable about friend August's crayfish romanticism is his ruthless combination of crayfish with eel — my own sense of decorum would not allow the crayfish, at the moment of demise on my table, to meet perhaps its very worst enemy (next to man himself).

The heavenly crayfish

There is a tenuous link between crayfish — "cancer" — and the signs of the zodiac. But if the truth be known, by "Cancer" the Romans meant all manner of crustaceans, and neither Romans nor Greeks rated the crayfish all that high as a delicacy. Instead it ranked as a "scavenger" — a denigrated category in all ages. Recipes in Roman cookery books mainly referred to lobsters. And in the

There were many things in Sweden a hundred years ago which August Strindberg denounced and detested, but never a harsh word did he say about crayfish. On the contrary — at the very mention of them his pen turned lyrical and his voice softened.

* The cruel way in which the vikings killed king Ella of Northumbria.

illuminated books of hours from medieval France, for example, the position of "cancer" is invariably occupied by a large edible crab.

Crayfish as medicine

No, the heyday of the crayfish in Europe did not dawn until the Dark Ages. And even then, the aversion to eating crayfish was so persistent up here in the far north that, understandably, they are not even mentioned as food until April 1504, when they were dished up in Copenhagen by Queen Christina of Denmark who at that time had a German chef, who was familiar with crayfish. This absence of recorded mention has prompted the question whether Sweden had any crayfish at all before the 16th century. Linnaeus, for example, believed them to have been planted by our Renaissance monarchs, but he was quite wrong. If he had boned up more on medieval Swedish literature, he would have seen, for example, that the crayfish was a part of military imagery – a breast plate, undeniably reminiscent of the crayfish's armoured thorax, could actually be termed *kräveta* (old spelling of kräfta: crayfish). But eating crayfish was out of the question.

On the other hand, crayfish are mentioned all the more frequently in medieval and Renaissance times as medicine. Specially pulverised "crayfish stones" (those tiny hemispherical formations to be found, especially at the beginning of the season, close to the crayfish's stomach) were regarded as something of a panacaea, e.g. for rabies and plague, dysuria and oedema, and whole crayfish stones were even used for stopping teeth. They were also propped under the eyelid if you had got something in your eye. Presumably this hurt so much that the original discomfort was forgotten: perhaps the stone had the practical benefit of causing a flow of tears copious enough to flush out the foreign body. Even in our own century, eye specialists have had to treat patients whose vision has been damaged by this rough treatment.

Why were the northerners so averse to the eating of crayfish? There may have been one perfectly rational reason: crustaceans quickly become deleterious, and they do not travel well. As recently as the 19th century, crustacean poisoning was a frequent cause of death in Sweden. Things were not exactly improved by the expedient of preservative treatment with arsenic, for example.

But perhaps there was also a biblical background to this dislike of crustaceans. In Leviticus we read: "Whatsoever hath more feet among all creeping things that creep upon the earth, them ye shall not eat," and crayfish certainly have "more feet" – no fewer than ten. I should imagine, though, that the aversion to crayfish and other "creeping things" is older than Christianity, so heartily were they detested by the common people. Ordinary people (and in this they were corroborated by Linnaean terminology) regarded crayfish as a kind of insect, and insects are something which we westerners refuse to eat on any account – they are, quite simply, "disgusting".

Crayfish stones used to be on sale in dispensaries, and they were used not only for getting things out of people's eyes but – pulverised – by nature healers as a cure for things like stitch, headache, the stone and even syphilis – probably with little success. But powdered crayfish stone as a cure for heartburn may not have been completely off target.

A crayfish is pictured in Dialogus creaturarum moralizatus (1483), the very first book printed in Sweden. It is shown swimming with a frog, and we are told that the frog, finding the crayfish dirty and ugly, wanted to get rid of it. When the crayfish, true to habit, swam backwards, the frog, thinking it frightened it, rashly jumped up to it, whereupon the crayfish pinched him in half with its claws. This, the author explains, teaches us, like the crayfish, to shun conflict and contention but, when attacked, to defend ourselves manfully. In the "nature study" books of the Middle Ages, every creature had its imaginary but morally significant characteristics.

... and as a penance

This theological aspect, however, does not appear to have embarrassed continental ecclesiastics, for the culinary beginnings of the crayfish were monastic. Monks and nuns had many problems during fasting seasons and searched high and low for substitutes for the meat that was denied them. Fish, on the other hand, was "fair game", and so the trick lay in stretching the term as far as possible. Beavers, seal and whales, for example, were blithely classified by the Church as fish, because they flourished in water. Vast numbers of crayfish were consumed during Lent. The records of one Bavarian monastery showed the monks there getting through more than 30,000 crayfish in a year. With such a diet in prospect, even the present writer might feel that monastic life had something to offer.

Crayfish eating spread soon enough from the cloister to other parts of medieval Germany, and the earliest German cookery books show that by the 15th century crayfish concoctions were a common ingredient of at least the upper class diet. And this, in a manner of speaking, was also the making of the delicacy in Sweden.

The crayfish in Renaissance Sweden

One of the earliest Swedish references to crayfish is a recipe from 1522, in which Bishop Peter Månsson, a man of many parts and Sweden's first scientist worthy of the name, recommended crayfish dissolved in schnapps as a cure for cholera. Only forty years later we find King Erik XIV urging one of his bailiffs to lose no time in sending him as many crayfish as could be found in the vicinity of Nyköping Castle:

"Know thou, Jöran Jönsson, that we both for our own needs and likewise for the foreign lords now visiting us need a goodly quantity of crayfish. It is moreover essential that a store of the same be laid up against the wedding feast which we purpose to hold presently. It is therefore our wish and command that you have them fished for in all places!"

Erik's successor on the throne, Johan III, not content with ordering his Kalmar bailiff to catch crayfish, required him to start farming them in the moats of Kalmar Castle. Now both these monarchs had something quite different in mind from medicine for cholera. What had happened?

Erik XIV was not only Sweden's first genuine Renaissance king in matters of culture and politics, he also made a genuine effort to refine the manners of a rather primitive royal court. His determination to move with the times applied, not least, to dining rooms and kitchens.

During his reign, courtiers stopped wiping mouths and fingers on the table cloth, and began using napkins instead. Wooden platters were discarded and people began eating off plates of pewter. And the king's kitchens were run by cooks he had brought in from Germany, for at that time the German cuisine was paramount in northern Europe. Among other things

The moat of Kalmar Castle, scene of Sweden's first crayfish farm, started by King Johan III, evidently a devoted crayfish eater. These crayfish, though, must have been pretty shortlived, considering what went into the moat from the castle.

In the mid-16th century, Olaus Magnus, Sweden's last Catholic Archbishop, now leading the life of an exile in Italy, wrote a superb description of Scandinavia. The picture reproduced here shows Nordic foxes cunningly fishing for crayfish with their tails. But look at the fox on the left. What does it hold in its mouth, if not a bunch of grass? Why? Because it combines crayfishing with delousing. Slowly it descends into the water and, as the water rises through its fur, the lice climb further and further up till, finally, only the fox's snout protrudes above the water, and all the minute parasites have taken refuge on the blades of grass, as illustrated. The fox lets go of the grass and the vermin are consigned to a watery grave. Which perhaps goes to show that the tales of the Archbishop are to be taken with a pinch of salt.

the German cooks brought the message that crayfish were edible. As should be clear from the Royal decrees already quoted, the innovation caught on both quickly and thoroughly in our country, once our rulers had acquired a taste for it. Not that crayfish were eaten whole, the way they are today. Far from it: the meat was extracted from the tails and used for minces and stews. Whole boiled crayfish are not mentioned in Sweden until the 17th century.

During the reign of Erik XIV, Olaus Magnus, the last Catholic Archbishop of Uppsala and now an exile in Italy, wrote "The History of the Northern Peoples", his magnum opus. In it he explained to astonished contemporaries how Swedish foxes go about catching crayfish.

"To catch crayfish, the fox walks to and fro along the shore with his tail dipped in the water. Lured by this rare sight, the crayfish flock round and, on their thus having entangled themselves in the hairs, he soon pulls them up. I have myself among the rocks of Norway seen a fox which dipped its tail in the water between the rocks and pulled up several crayfish, which he then devoured." Pull the other one, Your Grace!

Fancy a crayfish sausage?

Just now I mentioned Linnaeus' aversion to all shellfish. This is reflected not least by his lectures on diet, but there are several references in his writings which show quite clearly that he was

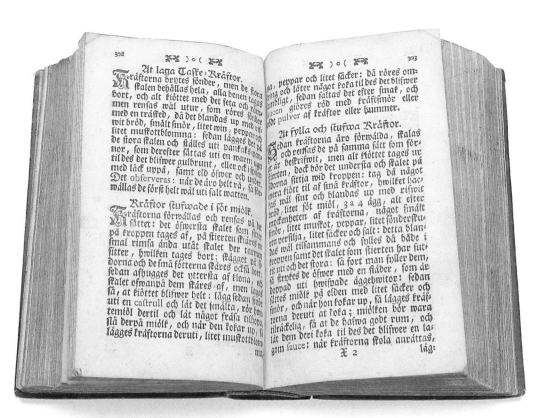

Kajsa Warg, the classical 18th century cookery writer, gives a full dozen recipes for crayfish, to wit:
Crayfish stewed in sweet milk (see illustration)
Crayfish to fill and stew
Petits patés of crayfish
Small poupetons of crayfish
A fine ragout of crayfish
Crayfish pudding
Crayfish cake
Crayfish sausage
Crayfish butter
Crucian carp stuffed with crayfish tails
Crayfish soup.

The great Linnaeus was no lover of crayfish. In his lectures on diet he said that insects were not for human consumption, and this category, his revolutionary biological system notwithstanding, he took to include the polypod shellfish.

allergic to shellfish: they gave him nettle rash. No wonder, then, that he pronounced them inedible.

Happy to record, not many people agreed with him. The gentry of 18th century Sweden loved shellfish and would not give them up for anything. Kajsa Warg and her contemporaries in the catering business had a much wider repertoire of crayfish meals than present-day cookery writers. Kajsa herself, for example, recommends crayfish buns and crayfish puddings, crayfish cake and crayfish soup – recipes which would indeed be tempting to experiment with but at the same time prohibitively expensive, so that on the whole we can only guess at what they tasted like.

But if I had good crayfish water of my own, I think I would go for the worthy Kajsa's "crayfish sausage", despite the glorious opening words of the recipe: "Parboil three score crayfish and clean out all the flesh." One then proceeds to grind the flesh, mix it with soaked wheaten bread, five eggs, butter, parsley, pepper, nutmeg, thyme and basil, salting the mixture and packing it into casings of sheep's gut, after which the sausages are boiled in milk to which plenty of butter has been added. When ready, the (chipolata-size) sausages have to be coated with crayfish butter and grilled. Who can imagine what they would taste like? Certainly not unpalatable!

The fondness of the 18th century upper classes for crayfish was not a passing fad, it stemmed from the new eating habits introduced by the Renaissance and subsequently refined by the French cuisine. As a result, crayfishing eventually became an im-

18th and 19th century cooks in manor houses and in the homes of the monied classes, when preparing delicious patés, aspics and jellies, would put them to set or bake in copper moulds displaying the type of raw material used. This early 19th century mould, in the Nordic Museum, Stockholm, ought logically to have been used for dishes described by Kajsa Warg by such names as "Petits patés of crayfish" or "Small poupetons of crayfish".

portant sideline in many Swedish districts, but do not suppose for a moment that "the common people" themselves would eat what they caught. No, crayfish were food for the gentry, like mushrooms, and that was that.

Now the "noble crayfish" of northern Europe is aromatically far superior to its continental relatives, and so in time crayfishing also became an important export business. From Lake Hjälmaren especially, salted crayfish tails were sent by the barrel, for example, to luxury restaurants in Germany, and already in the 1870s another Swedish cookery writer, Dr Hagdahl, trembled at the thought of Swedish crayfish being exterminated by overfishing. He was only too right. It is sad to think how one of our foremost culinary assets was almost wiped out, though in the event this was due more to "crayfish plague" (parasitic mould) than to trapping. A hundred years ago, Sweden was the leading European exporter of crayfish. Today we are far and away the biggest importer and are gradually helping to threaten the survival of crayfish in the new countries to which we turn with this unique craving of ours.

During the 1820s, Kajsa Warg's cookery book was superseded in middle-class Swedish kitchens by Margaretha Nylander's "Manual of Fine Cooking", which does not deign to mention anything so simple as boiled crayfish. On the other hand she does recommend crayfish in pea soup (!), crayfish patés and crayfish sauce with a joint of veal, not forgetting crayfish tails served with scrambled eggs or marinated in vinaigrette sauce.

The third Swedish classic of the cookery bookshelf, Dr Hag-dahl, was the first writer to explain the procedure for boiling cray-fish, added to which he presented about 25 different and more sophisticated ways of preparing them, e.g. as stuffing and decora-tion for roast pigeon.

Females hot or cold?

The story so far should not be taken to imply that crayfish parties with schnapps and silly hats by the light of smiling paper moon lanterns have been a regular feature of Swedish living ever since the 16th century. Far from it. In olden days, when crayfish were eaten *au naturel*, then as a rule they would be freshly cooked and warm. In a song on the subject, the late 18th century poet Carl Michael Bellman talks about people "harpooning" red cray-fish in the saucepan – for the simple reason that it was too hot to put your hand in. Hagdahl too recommended serving crayfish warm. Not many Swedes today have any idea what a delicacy they are missing out on. On one occasion, nearly 50 years ago now, I was amazed by being served, in the Finnish town of Nyslott, with freshly boiled crayfish. Once having learned to tackle them with-out getting blisters, I soon became a convert to the method (which requires more salt and dill in the cooking water). It was also in Finland, incidently, that I learned to let the little creatures spend their last hours rather like snails in the same situation: you put them in the bath in a decimetre of water and then pour on a

One classical way of arranging crayfish, Norway lobsters and lobs-ters is in the form of what the Swedes call a "crayfish bush" ("Buisson" in French). Both well-to-do homes and exclusive restaurants used to have a framework of the kind shown here, over which the shellfish would be hung, tail up, to form a pyramid, at the top of which there would be placed, like a flag or weather vane, a small skewer with a thick slice of truffle and a crayfish or a few big shrimps impaled on it. A "bush" like this would be served with mayon-naise or ravigotte sauce, in which case the crayfish would be boiled without dill (a herb not commonly used in French cooking).

From about the turn of the century right down to the present day, crayfish parties have engendered all manner of accessories, some of them for the moment, like hats and bibs, and others intended for long-term use, such as crayfish services and crayfish knives, serving dishes and schnapps glasses. Specially elegant ceramic crayfish motifs were cultivated by the big china factories, while the more burlesque variants, like these two dishes, often came from smaller workshops. The one with the frog in the middle is from Axel Elfstrand of Sjöbo in Skåne (Scania), southern Sweden. The shellfish are made in plaster moulds and positioned on a yellow and white surface which is patterned by scraping away part of the slip. The crayfish are earthenware red and the frog glazed black and green (diameter: 29 cm).

The crayfish dish with a central relief of a man laughing was made by Carl Lundholm, a potter at Furulund, Skåne, round about the turn of the century. It is surrounded by the inscription "The crayfish that I serve you will have all been boiled in the best of dill". The rim of the dish is set with twelve pressed, reddish-brown-glazed crayfish. The green-glazed bottom is splashed with blue and brown (diameter: 37.5 cm).

couple of litres of milk. This loosens their bowels, thereby sparing finnicky people like myself the task of picking away the excrement while eating. But at some point between Bellman and Strindberg, at the same time as arrack punch came to be served ice cold instead of hot, the Swedes altered the temperature of their crayfish, and this, coupled with the summer cottage and archipelago romanticism of the late Oscarian 19th century (for those who could afford it), gave rise to the typical Swedish crayfish party, with its peripheries and — sadly — its excessive doses of schnapps. Crayfish and schnapps, admittedly, belong together, but for my own part I treat the dram virtually as a kind of mouth water, its task being, together with the cheese on crisp bread, to reset the taste buds for a moment and prepare the palate for the next gust of crayfish aroma. People who drink themselves silly at crayfish parties might just as well be served fish fingers halfway through the party. For in their case it is perfectly true that "American crayfish are just as good as Swedish ones."

A party given by the bureaucrats

In earlier times, the eating of crayfish was not primarily confined to August: crayfish were available all the year round. But when crayfishing became big business (five million were caught in Lake Hjälmaren every year!) it was time to protect them from extermination, especially while they were changing shells and spawning. County by-laws were adopted during the 19th centu-

At the same time as there are perfectly authentic coats of arms featuring crayfish, like the one on the right reproduced from Jost Amman's "Wappen- und Stammbuch" (1589), send-ups of aristocracy and heraldry soon came to include their own variations on the theme. One skit of this kind is the "Adlerstop coat of arms", now part of the Bellman Collection at the Stockholm City Museum (but the property of the National History Museum). It displays the coat of arms granted by Bellman to one Mr Adlerstop ("Eagle tankard"), in reality a drink-sodden baker, whose emblem the poet described as follows:

In the scarlet field a pewter pot gleams and up on the lid an eagle rears.
In the midst of the shield the sunshine gleams and within the sun a crayfish appears.
Down below is a whale, it seems, and clenched in its maw the legend "Cheers!"

ry, generally prohibiting crayfishing from April to the beginning of August, and eventually nationwide regulations were introduced, making the period between 1st November and 8th August a closed season, which it remained until very recently. In this way, just for once, the authorities laid the foundations of a festive occasion, the most quintessentially Swedish of institutions – even more so than the Maypole – namely the crayfish party at the beginning of August. Although crayfish, admittedly, deepfrozen, are now to be had all the year around, most people still think of them as the culinary climax of the month of August. It certainly feels odd, having to round off this chapter with a word of commendation for one of the most dreadful of human inventions – bureaucracy. But, let credit be given where credit is due, even if it goes against the grain rather.

The crayfish of Småland are of long-standing repute and have not yet been entirely eliminated by "crayfish plague". The antiquity of the link between crayfish and the people of Småland is borne out, for example, by the crayfish in this seal of the ancient Tjust Hundred. The Tjust district, with its many small forest meres, was no doubt a happy hunting ground for crayfishers in times gone by, just as today. The crayfish symbol was revived and doubled by the Municipality of Gladhammar, in the Tjust district, for a municipal coat of arms adopted in 1953. But that only lasted until 1971, when the municipality merged with Västervik.

The crayfish, "Cancer", it will be recalled, was one of the "signs" of these zodiac-symbols of the galaxies, each of which "governed" one slice of the pie, a twelfth of the night sky and a twelfth of the year – a superstition which is still good business for many weekly magazines with horoscopes. (The illustration shows the earth, seasonal activities and the signs of the zodiac. The crayfish is at top left. Ann Rodan Picture Library.)

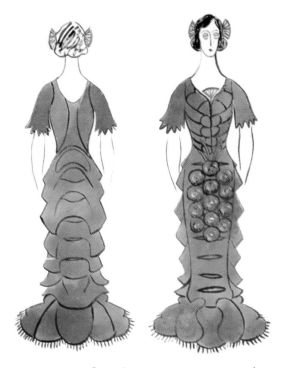

Crayfish crave these drinks!

Probably no Swedish artist produced more work featuring crayfish than Albert Engström. Most famous of all are the crayfish adorning his emphatic No! poster for Sweden's prohibition referendum in 1922.

Prohibitionist posters, with their starving children and battered wives of drunkards, stood little chance against Engström's simple but pungent slogan. And so it came about that the crayfish, for the first and perhaps last time ever, had a hand – well, claw – in the making of Swedish history.

Albert Engström was a frequent visitor at Harg, the home of the Beck-Friis family and not far from his own Grisslehamn, and his visits frequently coincided with the crayfish season. He willingly drew vignettes in the visitor's book, and reproduced here is a veritable mega-crayfish from 13th January 1936 (a bit late for a crayfish party), accompanied by a series of very blue-blooded names. On another occasion, using the pseudonym of Albert Patou, he produced an exceedingly refined crayfish party creation for his hostess, Baroness Beck-Friis.

Uppermost in the memories of ordinary Swedish people, though, are his killingly funny cartoons, in which, once again, the crayfish is a recurrent theme.

Editorial note: The Swedes voted 49% for prohibition and 51% against.

The glorious 8th of August!

After a few years in early life spent working with bookworms, both human and animal, at the Royal Library in Stockholm, Bosse Persson migrated to the gramophone industry. On-the-spot pressurisation of overworked producers resulted in one or two of his own lyrics getting, not only into the recording studio but into Sweden's top ten as well.

Things became really glamorous when film bosses began holding out money-dripping contracts. Two film sequences, one of 6 and the other of 29 seconds' duration, were just about completed before the film boss's daughter diverted her glamour to another target.

After nearly 40 years in Stockholm, 15 of them with the recording company, Bosse moved to Malmö. There, on the prospective continental bridge abutment, he stayed in the music business, but this time with SMC, Sweden's biggest record club.

Just over ten years ago he resigned as editor of the SMC membership journal, exchanging his typewriter for a word processor with the Görman Group, but continuing to write for the record club. In addition, his ten years with the Görman Group have given him the opportunity of writing about everything from bow saws and cheese doodles to open-air theatre and ... first-night crayfish parties.

The moon was in full bloom and wholesaler A.P. Bärnström squinted at it in search of some resemblance to the paper moon he had purchased earlier that day in early August, 1932.

He had spotted the brightly coloured paper moon in a shop window emblazoned with the device: "Modern people deck the crayfish table with Almedahl's crayfish adornments". Surrounding the suspended legend were a number of lunar caricatures in lambent yellow and red. The hand-written docket dangling on a string from the apple-cheeked moon proclaimed: "... make a romantic decoration for your crayfish supper. Only 95 öre!"

"Well, why not?" he had thought to himself: "A spot of romance never did any harm."

In earlier years he had enjoyed the first night of the crayfish season in a civilised manner at the Royal Opera Restaurant in Stockholm, but this year he had finally given in to his wife's powers of persuasion and promised to honour his sister-in-law and brother-in-law with his presence at a crayfish supper at the allotments.

After further negotiations with his wife he had actually consented to assist brother-in-law Gustav with the actual trapping of the first-night animals.

So here he was, beneath the original version of his coloured lanterns, heading, together with Gustav Palmsparre, his brother-in-law, for Gustav's crayfish water. Just a few hours earlier they had

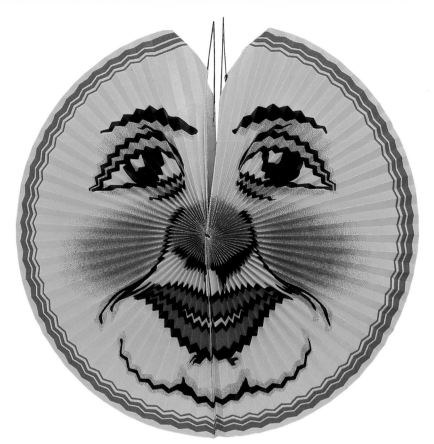

Even the man in the moon is available in various moods, ranging from the big smile to gentle melancholy. The latter with a gaze suggesting that he has seen and heard it all before. Nothing can surprise this gentleman anymore – not even a Swedish crayfish party.

arrived at the brother-in-law's allotment chalet, and while A.P. gathered strength for the night's exertions, Gustav had got out 20 or so crayfish traps and loaded them onto a hand cart.

"Do you have to walk so fast?" he pleaded, when Gustav, who was pulling the loaded cart, stepped up the pace. "I can't keep up, pushing this thing."

After stopping for breath, at A.P.'s insistent request, halfway down to Gustav's jetty, they had finally covered the 700 metres, taking their cages and bait with them.

"I'll bait up while you get your breath back," said Gustav.

A.P. sat down on the jetty, his feet just above the water, while Gustav unloaded the traps. When all the cone-shaped traps were in position on the jetty, he went back to the cart for a pail.

"Apologies for the slight pong, but crayfish crave these fragrances before reversing into paradise."

"There ought to be a law against it," said A.P., wrinkling his nose. "Are you going to poison them or something?"

"Flayed frogs are the ideal thing," said Gustav, "but now they'll have to make do with rabbit." He began poking through the roof opening of the traps at the noisome gobbets inside. "Next to tender frog's meat, rancid rabbit is the best thing to give them."

"Brother-in-law, please!" came the protest loud and clear. "If you don't leave off I'll be seasick."

"Well come and be seasick on board," said Gustav. "You sit in the stern and I'll pass you the traps."

Big picture, pages 22-23
The "The glorious 8th of August!" episode does not take place in this setting – an allotment area somewhere in Sweden. But it could very well have done so. Sweden in summertime is blessed with innumerable ready-made settings for crayfish festivities.

To begin with, the crayfish party was purely a family occasion, or at least reserved for the family and its closest friends, with a corresponding relaxation of "protocol".

A.P. hesitated but took courage, jumping down into the flat-bottomed rowing boat with unexpected agility. Gustav handed down the traps, now baited, in rapid succession before jumping down into the boat himself.

"We're only going a little way," he said, casting off. "We'll just let the boat drift along the shore and we'll put down one cage every 20 metres or so. How many crayfish did you plan on eating?"

"Twenty," came the snappy but nasal reply, A.P.'s nose being tightly squeezed between thumb and forefinger.

"So with eight of us we'll need seven or eight score just about," Gustav surmised. "Three trips should do it. First trap away!"

Still keeping a tight hold of his nose, A.P. heaved the first cage overboard with his spare hand.

"Stop and belay, Brother-in-law!" Gustav shouted. "We don't want to batter the crayfish to death before cooking them!"

To show what he meant he himself took the next trap, carefully pushing it down below the water. Once again, A.P. Bärnström summoned up courage, let go of his nose and lowered the third cage so gently to the lake bed that hardly a ripple could be seen on the surface of the water.

"Well done, thou good and faithful servant," said Gustav, lowering the fourth. "We're doing fine."

Half an hour later all 20 traps had been set and the red cork floats were bobbing gently in a long line parallel to the water's edge, clearly visible in the bright moonlight.

"Right, back we go for rest and recovery," said Gustav, poling them back to the jetty with one oar.

Once ashore, A.P. felt better and when Gustav fetched a basket, containing coffee and sandwiches, from the hand cart, life became really worth living.

"Any chance of a wee snifter?" he inquired discreetly, with a sidelong glance at the basket.

There certainly was, and although Gustav had perhaps taken that bit about the snifter being a wee one just a little too literally, A.P. still sighed with contentment after emptying the screw cap of its golden brown liquid.

About eight screw caps later, it was time to clear the table, as it were, and have a look to see whether the crayfish had also dined well.

"All aboard!".

This time Gustav took the oars, skilfully heading for the first float. The delicacies in trap number one had attracted six takers.

A.P. quite aghast, clapped his hand over his mouth and, slowly removing it, whispered in a trembling voice: "Gustav, Gustav. May the Chamber of Commerce have mercy on us, but now you've got that wretched crayfish plague here as well…"

"Plague? What on earth do you mean, Brother-in-law dear? They look perfectly healthy to me."

"But can't you see, Gustav? They're black all over…"

A.P. took some convincing that the crayfish would change co-

The crayfish also makes an excellent pretext for throwing a really big party for all the family's friends or all the firm's employees.

A crayfish party record was set during the 1986 Malmö festival, when nearly 10,000 people gathered in the main square got through more than 90,000 crayfish, drank beer, as well as stronger things of their own purchasing, and had the time of their lives. This rated a mention in the Guiness Book of Records. Since then the party has been an annual event – I should think so too!

lour when they got into hot water. "Just like politicians, then," he muttered, while Gustav emptied the trap and carefully deposited the crayfish in the pail.

The next trap contained just one crayfish, the third was completely empty.

"If we go on like this we won't even make two score," said A.P. grumpily, but when he pulled up trap number four there were another six crayfish for Gustav to put in the pail.

"You musn't be so impatient," he said. "If we go on like this, with more than four per cage on average, we'll finish sooner than I thought."

When all twenty traps had been emptied, the average of four crayfish per trap proved to be an underestimate and they returned to the jetty with the pail brimming over.

"See what I mean?" said Gustav, retrieving a big wooden box from the hand cart and emptying the pail into it. "95 crayfish already and the night is still young!"

The second tour of the traps gave only another 20 crayfish, but after the third, just as Gustav had predicted, the catch now stood at 164.

"This will keep Ida and Vera busy when they arrive", said Gustav, thinking of their wives, who would be arriving by bus the following morning. "All we have to do is make sure of getting in wood and water and putting up the tables in the bower."

"And sleeping," said A.P.

Mr Bärnström's contribution to the crayfish party included the classical moon-shaped crayfish lanterns which already existed in the 1930s. Before much longer he could also have contributed both crayfish hats and crayfish bibs with ready-printed schnapps ditties. So there is something in what a wise man once said, namely that the crayfish party is a children's party for grown-ups.

They arrived back at Gustav's and Vera's allotment chalet on the dot of three and five minutes later A.P. was fast asleep on the kitchen sofa, leaving Gustav to unload the three boxes of crayfish from the handcart and carry them into the kitchen. Putting down the third box, he couldn't keep himself from lifting the lid and peeping inside at the catch.

"Now have a good rest," he said to them, "and don't disturb His Lordship. Tomorrow we're going to have a party!"

The morning bus arrived punctually at half past seven at the crossroads two kilometres away, and Gustav was waiting there with his hand cart.

"Lucky you brought the hand cart," said his wife, Vera. "There's no end of stuff to carry on a day like this."

"Yes, and these are the crayfish plates," said Ida, helping Gustav to manoeuvre a big cardboard box onto the hand cart. "Father-in-law said that we could borrow them if we promised not to break any. But where's my old man, then? Did he catch any crayfish last night?"

"He's asleep and we caught 164," Gustav replied. A.P. was still asleep when they got to the chalet, but by dint of united efforts they roused him and got him onto his feet. Still drowsy and in no condition to protest, he acquiesced for several hours in fetching water, bringing wood, fetching more water and bringing in more firewood.

We are not told so, but Mrs Ida Bärnström may very well have decorated her dress with a glittering crayfish brooch. Well, if she didn't, somebody else did.

Standing on the red-hot wood stove were two big copper preserving pans, one containing boiling water and the other a dill-fragrant liquid of some kind, and with growing amazement Mr Bärnström watched his normally so amiable wife callously and unhesitatingly transfer one crayfish after another to the boiling water. For every sixth crayfish thus consigned to a final swimming tour, she would pick up the whole batch from the boiling water, in a big perforated spoon, transferring them to the pan with the dill liquid. Then, after waiting for the water in the first pan to come to the boil again, she would start all over again with another six crayfish. By midday all 164 crayfish had turned from black to red and were now closely packed on their catafalque in the seething liquor. Mr Bärnström glanced wistfully in the direction of the sofa, but a discreet look from his wife made him realise in next to no time that repose was out of the question.

"Pour yourself a cup of coffee," she said, "and then you've got to help Gustav carry out tables and chairs to the bower. And when that's done you can help Vera to get out the crayfish service and wash it up, so that she can start laying the table, and then you can ..."

Although the list of things to be done was of Wagnerian proportions, everything was present and correct in time for the guests' arrival at 7 p.m. The Christmas lights in the coloured moon faces were lit, the long garland of hand-sized hearts was strung up right across the bower, and Mr Bärnström's wife had

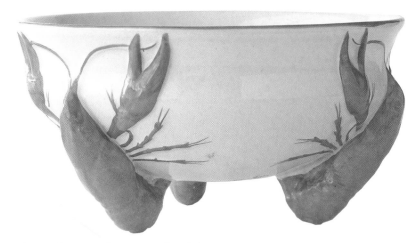

recovered from the shock of one of Father-in-law's valuable Rörstrand plates, with crayfish décor by Alf Wallander, slipping out of her husband's hands.

"I think we can stick it together," Vera consoled her while she and Ida were laying the table. "I hope the men have remembered to put the schnapps and the crate of beer to cool," she reminded herself while putting up the glasses, which were also decorated (painted) with crayfish.

They had remembered. Using – hopefully – stout cords they had lowered down both a crate of beer and a crayfish trap containing three various bottles of schnapps into the well.

One of the bottles was flavoured with Gustav's own patent mixture. "The trick," he said, "is to pick the wormwood on St. Bartholomew's Eve, then next year to submerge it in plain schnapps on St. Andrew's Day and drink it after the tenth Sunday after Trinity. It's at its best when the crayfish season begins. But now I think we'd better go and get changed."

Five minutes before the four guests arrived together by taxi from town, the two host couples were ready and waiting to welcome them. A.P., in a white dinner jacket, and Ida, with a musquash cape carelessly thrown over her shoulders, met them down at the gate.

First out of the car were Hans and his wife Greta. Hans, in charge of a department at the NK store in Stockholm, kissed

Over the years, the crayfish has provided both Sweden and foreign – mainly German – china factories with a decorative theme. This design, by Rörstrand's Alf Wallander, is a Swedish classic.

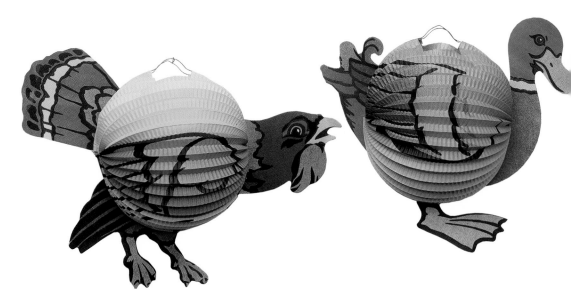

Ida's hand and presented her with a smartly wrapped parcel. After Douglas, with all the professional skill of a senior bank clerk, had rounded off the figure on the clock and shelled out accordingly, it was time for him and his wife Bettan to join in the huggings and kissings.

"Oh, how jolly this is!" Bettan giggled, kissing A.P. right on the mouth. "I simply adore the country!"

Both ladies put their arms through A.P.'s and the three of them headed the procession to the illuminated bower where Gustav and Vera were waiting with glasses of champagne for them.

"Well, how stylish!" said Bettan. "I simply adore bubbly."

"Well, cheers everyone, grand to see you", said A.P. "Welcome to our humble board. Plain and simple it may be, but by Jove we had to work for it."

They drank to each other and, while A.P. and Gustav made off to the well to haul up the schnapps and beer, Ida opened the parcel from Greta and Hans.

"How nice," she said, unfolding a lantern shaped like a portly pig, "but what is it?"

"I thought all this business with men in the moon is so trivial," said Greta. "Everybody has them nowadays, so I thought we'd be a bit different. Oh, what lovely moons you've hung up, by the way. Get another candle and we'll put the pig up as well. Hans, incidentally, thought it looked just a teeny weeny little bit like dear old A.P."

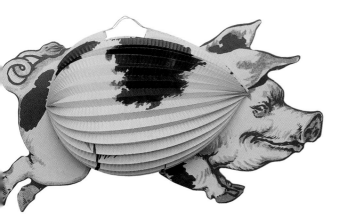

They drank to each other again and A.P. and Gustav returned to the bower with beer and schnapps.

"Now, empty your glasses and take your places," said Gustav, putting out a number of bottles of beer still wet from the well. "And just to be on the safe side, don't forget your bibs. They're nice ones – Vera cut them out of paper which she had scrounged at the grocer's back home."

"And here comes the star turn of the evening," shouted Vera, entering the bower with a great dishful of crayfish. "Eat as many as ever you can. Gustav was out all night catching them, so they're absolutely fresh."

"I think I prefer them dead," said Douglas, and Bettan went into peels of hysterical laughter.

"He's a card, our Douglas," she panted between bursts of laughter. "Prefer them dead! Isn't he wonderful?!"

"As a matter of fact, Anton also helped to catch the beastly things," Ida snapped, and her eyes produced a whole battery of icicles, launched in the direction of Vera.

Vera made herself as small as possible and Gustav jumped in to mediate:

"Yes of course A.P. was there. Fact is, I think we did about half each," he said. "Now, dig in everybody."

And while the dish, which just like the crayfish plates was from Rörstrand and decorated with imitation crayfish, went the rounds of the table, Gustav uncorked the beer bottles and poured out

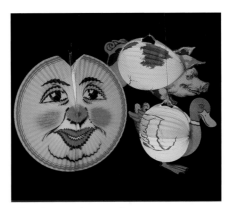

The classical paper lantern, guaranteeing a full moon for every Swedish crayfish party, is sometimes joined by less common designs, often birds of different kinds or, as shown here, a pig of rather mercantile aspect.

Designed for candle-lighting and often years of service.

The traditional schnapps can also be drunk from a glass which leaves no doubt as to who is being toasted.

The butter dish, inserted in an earthenware pot filled with cold water, comes in very handy on warm summer evenings, but people need to be told about it to avoid accidents!

the schnapps, which had cooled perfectly down in the well.

"Now," said Vera, "help yourselves to bread and cheese. The butter's in that little dish at the end of the table. Would you mind passing it, Douglas? But mind how you lift it…"

She was too late. Douglas upset all the water with which the outer dish had been filled to keep the insert and the butter cold.

"Blast," said Douglas, trying to dry himself with one of the lovely red napkins. "Blast again," on discovering that the napkin had stained his trousers red

"He's a card," said A.P., popping the first crayfish into his mouth. "Here's to a really smashing evening!"

"We've got to sing as well," Gustav interrupted him, bellowing forth a schnapps ditty with so much gusto that the candle in the pig went out.

"Have we come here to eat and booze or to sing?" said A.P., helping to refill the glasses as crayfish, drams of schnapps and songs succeeded one another.

A good few drams later, the mood had risen to carnival dizziness and Vera and Ida had taken turns, over and over again, at replenishing the supply of crayfish.

"Now ish bout time fnuther lill schong," said Gustav, striking up on his own again with all the persistence of a stuck gramophone needle.

"Oh, Gustav", Bettan sighed, turning her eyes heavenwards, "you've got a lovely singing voice."

"You should hear him decoying the female crayfish," said A.P. "He sounds ever so randy, fools them every time."

"Go on with you," said Bettan.

"How else do you think we caught all these lovely females?" A.P. replied, managing to look quite indignant about it. "Perhaps you think we just threw in some rancid rabbit meat to catch them with."

"Oh, please, Gustav," Bettan whispered, "let's hear it!"

"Indeed you won't," said Vera, "not while I'm still awake anyway. And besides, we've run out of crayfish."

Just then a motor horn sounded at the gate.

"Come on," said Hans, "that's our taxi come to collect us. So if you're ready, girls…"

During the final round of hugging and kissing, A.P. was unable to rise from his chair, but Greta and Bettan sat down on his generously proportioned knees to give him the treatment.

"We must do this again as soon as possible," said Douglas, and Hans agreed as they hugged Vera and Ida. "I suppose we ought to have helped with the washing up, but I'm afraid the car's waiting."

The two crayfishers were dead to the world and snoring in their chairs before the tail lights of the taxi had rounded the first bend in the road. The sisters looked to their sleeping heroes before putting a blanket over each of them.

"Thank goodness for some peace and quiet," said Ida. "I hope they sleep in tomorrow morning."

The party's over. Next day is clearing-up day for the hosts. Often, though, a thankfully simple procedure after a crayfish party. Ashtrays, if used, have to be emptied (or the floors swept). The thought came to us when we spotted this crayfish, which in fact is an ashtray. They don't make them like that anymore!

Equally hard to come by, presumably is a tankard like this Russian one, with the crayfish in person lending a helping hand to the thirsty.

A. Stellan Karlsson

Spoiled for choice

Linnaeus got it wrong

It was more by chance than design that A. Stellan Karlsson went in for crayfish farming. He began by reading civics, but then in 1968 – in a raffle – he won a vacation job as field assistant on a crayfish survey. After this he was hooked on aquaculture, which at that time was in its infancy.

Between 1967 and 1976 he took part in the Swedish expeditions to the USA in search of the crayfish from which new stocks were to be raised in Sweden.

In 1972 he became crayfish farm manager at Simontorp, and ten years later took over as managing director.

Linnaeus insisted that crayfish, being insects, should never be eaten. Today we know that he was wrong. Crayfish ought definitely to be eaten and they're not insects, they are *arthropods*. So too, admittedly, are spiders and insects, but crayfish constitute a class in their own right – *Crustacea*. There are many crustaceans, over 25,000 species. Some of them belong to the Decapoda order, and this is where we find such delicate crustaceans as the crab, the lobster and the freshwater crayfish.

There are some 500 species of freshwater crayfish, fairly evenly distributed worldwide. It may perhaps come as a surprise that the African mainland has never had an endemic crayfish, whereas Madagascar has one species of its own, which moreover has been

of great economic importance to the native population. The main emphasis of the present account will be on species occurring in the international market, in our kitchens and on our plates.

A crayfish by any other name...

By tradition, crayfish have been blessed with a variety of mind-stirring names. Noble Crayfish, Signal Crayfish, Edelkrebs, Yabby, Marron and Red Swamp Crawfish for example. Harder selling of frozen crayfish in recent years has further confused things with neologisms like Turkish mountain lake crayfish, American river crayfish and Jazz crayfish. Since, however, the differences of flavour and consistency are just as great between crayfish species

As a result of that raffle ticket in 1968, A. Stellan Karlsson has become a leading authority in aquaculture and is internationally in demand as a consultant and lecturer. So far his assignments have taken him to 30 or more countries.

Between 1981 and 1984 he was President of the I.A.A. (International Association of Astacology).

Today he is managing director in charge of all activities at Simontorp, from crayfish to wild boar and blueberries.

His leisure, if any, is divided between hunting, fishing and photography.

Turkish or Long-clawed Crayfish
Astacus leptodactylus

Noble crayfish
Astacus astacus

as between different kinds of fish, it is important to try and see through the names, so as to ensure a plateful of what is really wanted.

The original, European crayfish species are only five in number *(Astacus astacus, Astacus leptodactylus, Astacus pachypus, Austropotamobius pallipes* and *Austropotamobius torrentium)*.

The international crayfish market really includes only two of these, namely the **Noble Crayfish** *(Astacus astacus)* and the **"Turkish" or Long-clawed Crayfish** *(Astacus leptodactylus).* *A. pallipes*, the **White-Clawed Crayfish**, occurs in the British isles, the north of Spain and the former Yugoslavia. *A. torrentium* is found, rather sparingly, in Central Europe. *A. pachypus* occurs in southeast Europe, north of the Black Sea.

An honest crayfish?

The Noble Crayfish — why "noble"? — is the original, northern European species. It is found in colder European waters and is sometimes imported, for example, from Finland, Norway, Poland and Greece.

In Sweden it is the most expensive of all species in the market, because of its outstanding culinary qualities, which are further accentuated by its coming, more often than not, from cool, clean waters. It does not exist outside Europe, however, and what we in Sweden call "American River Crayfish" (or "American Noble Crayfish") is something quite different.

Main illustration, pp. 36-37.
With big dams, islands and inlets, the crayfish can have fish, fowl and game for company.

When boiled, the Noble Crayfish turns a fine dark red. It has fairly big claws and a rather rough shell. Being the most expensive kind, it is nearly always marketed by its right name.

Not dishonest, but...

Astacus leptodactylus is sometimes referred to as the "**Turkish**" **or Long-clawed Crayfish**, though it also occurs in Poland, Lithuania, Latvia, Ukraine and Russia. Ever since Sweden began importing it in the 1960s, it has been packed in cartons with many different names on. Possibly this is because its culinary quality is greatly inferior to that of the Noble Crayfish, a fact which fanciful names like "Mountain Lake Crayfish" are intended to conceal.

The claws are conspicuously long and narrow. The shell is thin but spiky and the carapace is angular. The colour when boiled is pale red.

One of the first immigrants

After the "crayfish plague" had appeared in Europe in the 1860s, new stocks had to be planted, and the first to be tried was *Orconectes limosus*, introduced in 1890 from North America to Germany by a fish farmer called Max von dem Borne. Descendants of the 100 specimens he imported are now scattered all over Central Europe. This crayfish, known as **Kamberkrebs** in German, is small and hard to catch. Since, moreover, it accepts heavily polluted water, it is seldom if ever seen on the market.

Signal Crayfish
Pacifastacus leniusculus

Red Swamp Crayfish
Procambarus clarkii

The Noble Crayfish is dead, almost. Long live the Signal Crayfish!
By the end of the 1950s, with most of Sweden's crayfish waters knocked out by fungal disease and no signs of an improvement, the authorities began looking for a resilient substitute for the Noble Crayfish. Many different species were examined and a couple of American ones were secretly tested in a few Swedish lakes. Comparative studies proceeded in Sweden and the USA throughout the 1960s, until finally it was decided to introduce the Signal Crayfish into plague-ridden Swedish waters.

The first shipment landed in Malmö on Midsummer's Eve 1969. They had been caught in Lake Tahoe, California, and flown over packed in snow from Squaw Valley. Altogether that summer about 60,000 crayfish were airlifted across the Atlantic and released in 60 Swedish watercourses. After that, all imports of live crayfish were prohibited, and so all introductions since 1970 have employed Swedish-produced material. The scheme has been tremendously successful. About 700 tonnes of crayfish were caught in Sweden in 1993, at least 90 per cent of them Signal Crayfish. When the scheme began, the national catch was only a few score tonnes. Within a couple of years it will probably have reverted to the pre-plague level in 1907, about 1,000 tonnes!

A successful immigrant

Pacifastacus leniusculus was imported to Sweden and Finland in 1969 to colonise plague-ridden lakes. In Sweden it was dubbed the **Signal Crayfish**, a name which caught on in the rest of Europe. It originated in the north-west of the USA, but introductions have now given it a much wider habitat. More than 20 European countries now have Signal Crayfish populations, and in Sweden this is the dominant species.

The Signal Crayfish has a smooth, fairly hard shell which turns bright red when boiled, though not quite so red as that of the Noble Crayfish. It gets its name from the pale spot on the hinge of its claw. The claw itself is big and wide.

A Red Swamp Crayfish – by another name!

Another American species introduced in Europe is *Procambarus clarkii*, the Red Swamp Crayfish. This was introduced in the south of Spain during the early 1970s and now sells in large numbers in Sweden. It is packaged under more fanciful names. *Procambarus* has a fairly hard shell with sharp hooks. When boiled it turns a beautiful deep red. Alive it is black nearly all over, with red hooks. (There is in fact another American crayfish which was inadvertently imported to Spain with *P. clarkii*, namely *P. acutus*, the **White River Crawfish**, but this is much rarer in Spain, never occurs in pure stocks and, consequently, is little seen in our kitchens.)

In addition to the Signal Crayfish and the Red Swamp Crayfish, America has another 300 or so species. All of them have the same property which has made the Signal Crayfish so valuable, namely resistance to the crayfish plague. This is because the disease emanated from America, with the result that, over the centuries, the crayfish there have become immune to it.

Crayfish are not all that widely used in American cooking. They do figure in the north-west, in the old Scandinavian settlements round the Great Lakes and in the southern states, especially Louisiana, where crayfish are a big industry. This is the true home of *Procambarus clarkii*, the Red Swamp Crayfish, which is the world's most-farmed species. It grows very fast indeed, which is the main reason why it has been introduced in all continents but Australia. Its quality is rated (by us Europeans) lower than that of the Noble and Signal Crayfish, and so it comes very cheap. Outside the USA it is sold under all sorts of names except the right one.

...or another recipe

In its native Louisiana, the crayfish is prepared in quite a different way from in Europe and the result is a true delicacy. A Louisiana crayfish party is probably the most festive and succulent of human experiences. *Procambarus* is not at its best, on the other hand, in traditional Swedish recipes.

Pacifastacus, the ancestor of Swedish Signal Crayfish, is

Champion crayfish jockey
Stellan Karlsson, who wrote this section, is not only managing director of Simontorp Aquaculture and one of Sweden's leading experts on crayfish in general and Signal Crayfish in particular, but also a world champion in crayfish racing, a sporting event which is little known in Sweden but in the USA has quite a following, mainly in the eminent crustacean regions of Louisiana.

In a Crawfish Race each competitor personally chooses a crayfish which is given a suitable designation and then, together with an opponent, placed under a bucket in the middle of a large round table. At a sign from the referee, the bucket is removed and the crayfish make off in fairly unpredictable directions. The winner is the first one to reach and fall over the edge of the table.

On one of his visits to the USA, Stellan was invited to both the festivities and the competition taking place in Baton Rouge, Louisiana, as part of a local celebration of the favourite species. Though incompletely apprised of the qualities required of eventing crayfish, he carefully selected his own favourite and christened it "Clovisse of Sweden".

Cont. overleaf

To the astonishment of all concerned, "Clovisse of Sweden" won, first the heat, then the semifinal and then the final! Stellan Karlsson and "Clovisse of Sweden" were declared, with all due ceremony and with the plaque shown above, "Winner – 1st International Crawfish Race – Baton Rouge, LA. 1974".

Stellan and Clovisse had now automatically qualified for the world championship, to be held a little later in nearby Breaux Bridge, "Crawfish Capital of the World".

Unfortunately Stellan could not attend in person, but he asked a good friend to enter "Clovisse of Sweden" for him. This the friend did and once more the magnificent crayfish emerged victorious.

Unlike many other successful racing animals, "Clovisse of Sweden" was not sent to stud but spent her declining years in a special display aquarium at Louisiana State University, Baton Rouge, to her own gratification and that of all visitors.

caught in the north-west and, if properly treated afterwards, makes, in frozen form, a bargain alternative to fresh Swedish members of the same species.

There are many other crayfish species in North America which are serviceable in the kitchen, but these occur, at most, locally and not on the international crayfish market.

The odds are, however, that in future we will be making the acquaintance of a few more prolific species from the USA, such as *Orconectes spp.*

Guests from afar

In some years, Australian crayfish have appeared on European shop counters. This applies above all to the Yabby *(Cherax destructor)*, from south-eastern Australia, and the Marron *(Cherax tenuimanus)* from the south-west.

Yabbies are fairly similar to our crayfish in appearance, but they have stouter claws with short "fingers". When boiled the Yabby is pale red with touches of white/yellow. In quality the Yabby is looked on here in Europe as a cut above the American Red Swamp Crayfish, but a good deal inferior to the Signal and Noble Crayfish.

The Marron is sometimes sold as a freshwater lobster. It is much bigger than the European species, weights of 3-4 hg being quite usual. (But Australia has bigger crayfish still. Some specimens caught have been more than 70 cm long!)

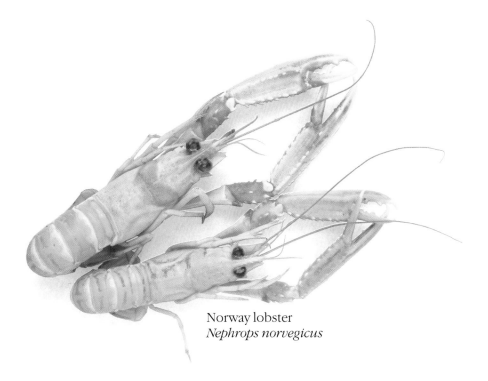

Norway lobster
Nephrops norvegicus

The Marron is often grilled and quality-wise it is quite superb, one of the most delicate of crustaceans. (As a result, the Marron is being sold for farming, especially in America. The buyer is not usually warned that it will die immediately on coming into contact with the crayfish plague, so understandably, the American farming ventures have been only moderately successful.)

But the likeliest Australian crayfish species for the market of the future is quite another one, namely *Cherax quadricarinatus*, known as Red Claw because its claw, even before boiling, has a bright red edge. Farmers have had their eye on this species for a number of years, and its future seems full of promise. It has not yet reached the European market, so its culinary value remains to be tested.

Not all fish is cod, so...

No doubt there are many other crayfish species which would be an asset to the kitchen but has not yet been utilised. There are latent resources in both Asia and South America. Unfortunately, though, the crayfish sold from other countries are nearly always of the same species, namely *Procambarus clarkii*, our old friend from Louisiana. The crayfish sold from Kenya, China, Costa Rica, Louisiana and Spain are all of the same species, which moreover has been introduced in at least another 30 countries besides. So shoppers have every reason to make a close study of the fine

In the sea as well
All these crayfish species live in freshwater. But there are marine species too, and one of them, for culinary reasons, is usually compared with freshwater crayfish, namely the Norway lobster, *Nephrops norvegicus*.

Norway lobsters, lobsters proper and crabs have free-floating larvae which do not resemble the adult animal, whereas the juveniles of freshwater crayfish resemble their parents from the very beginning. Despite these biological differences, the Norway lobster bears comparison with the freshwater crayfish as raw material for the kitchen.

Crayfish thrive best in river banks, and so professional growers often employ networks of dykes for maximum output.

print on the carton. The country of origin often provides a clue, but by no means always. The inclusion of the scientific name should also be stipulated. After all, would anybody shopping cod accept a package reading "Fish from Norway"?!

A little about the crayfish

As explained earlier, the crayfish is a *Decapod* ("ten-legs"). It has five pairs of walking legs, the first of which are equipped with big claws. The basic structure of the crayfish is quite the opposite of our own. We have an internal skeleton around which internal organs and tissues have been built up, whereas the crayfish has an outward shell surrounding its soft and sensitive parts. That shell consists mostly of calcium carbonate, and because it does not grow it has to be replaced as the crayfish becomes larger. While this is happening the crayfish is quite defenceless and cannot even eat, because its jaws also have to be replaced. (So it is not true that the crayfish eats up its own shell after changing – they eat up each other's!) The shell is able to harden because the crayfish has built up, in advance, a store of Gastroliths (crayfish stones). These stones, two per crayfish, are dissolved after the change of shell, and the calcium thus released is used for the hardening process.

Many people consider the females to be the superior delicacy, the reason being that in the commonest fishing season, August, their ovaries are full of roe. The ovaries are located dorsally, just in front of the edge of the carapace. (The males have their spermatic ducts in roughly the same place, and towards the end of the crayfishing season these come to resemble small white balls of wool, prompting suspicions of worm on the part of inexperienced crayfish eaters. The phenomenon, then, is perfectly natural and harmless, though not very appetising to look at.) Picking out the females from a mound of crayfish is pretty easy. They are always relatively wider across the tail than the males, and can be said to be widest over the hips – whereas a male is widest over the shoulders. (In doubtful cases one can turn the crayfish over and look at its belly side. The males have, right at the front of their tails, an extra pair of legs – small, white, forward-pointing – which serve as copulatory organs.)

A word about colour

The colouring of the shell is made up of red, yellow, green, brown and blue pigments. The green, brown and blue ones cannot tolerate heat, so after boiling only the red and yellow ones remain, and the crayfish turns an appetising shade of red.

Lastly, although the crayfish can reverse and swim backwards if threatened, it normally walks – forwards.

Anders Salomonsson

Catching crayfish —
a multi-stage ritual

Anders Salomonsson is Associate Professor of Ethnology at Lund University and at present is working as Director of the Ethnology Archives in Lund.

He has at various times been both school teacher, museologist and researcher. He has researched and written about food as a cultural manifestation and, not surprisingly therefore his doctoral thesis was entitled: "The Small Beer of Gotland. Culture as a symbol of regional identity". As the author and co-author of books on food and eating habits, he has vigorously highlighted the importance of diet in cultural development.

Even though the farmers of yesteryear did not catch crayfish for their own tables, they sold them to others. The buyers were town dwellers who, as the farmer saw it, had bad enough taste to ingest these weird creatures. Gradually, more and more townspeople themselves took part in the catching of crayfish, and the letting of crayfish waters became a welcome sideline for many country people.

The tackle

Crayfish can be caught in many ways. The easiest way is to take them by artificial light in the evening or at night. This used to be done with a flare or lantern, nowadays a torch is used. The fisher-

man walks gingerly through the water alongside the bank, picking up the crayfish he sees.

Fishing with a bag net is also a fairly direct sort of method. The bag net consists of a metal ring – withy in olden days – with a net attached to it. The bait is secured in the middle and the net is lowered into the water and, with the aid of a line, positioned level on the bed. When the crayfish are thought to have spotted the bait and crept up onto the net, the bag is quickly retrieved.

A crayfish trap is made of steel wire or withies and netting. It looks like an inverted, tapered basket with a flat bottom and a hole at the very top. The wire cage is similarly constructed but has at least two openings at the sides and, unlike the trap, does

Anders is Chairman of the International Ethnological Food Research Association, Secretary of the Skåneland Gastronomical Academy and a contributor to the Swedish National Encyclopedia.

With the mist wafting over the water on a summer's night, it's time to empty the crayfish traps!

not have a flat bottom. Consequently it does not have to be positioned so carefully and, unlike the withy trap, does not have to stand on a flat surface.

Fishing waters

Fishing waters can be of greatly varying character. Small lakes and forest tarns are perhaps the commonest, and waters of this kind are often fished from a boat. My own experiences of crayfishing come from a Småland river with blackish-brown water and water lilies.

As a child and teenager I went crayfishing all through the fifties and halfway through the sixties. I think it was 1950 (when I was four) that we went crayfishing for the first time in Stacka, some way south of Kalmar. Stacka was a typical mid-19th century village – a marginal community with a few crofts, a patchwork of small fields and a forge. By 1950 only one croft remained, with its cottage and tiny barn. The stony in-fields were returning to nature. The cottage was the home of two elderly, now retired, crofters – man and wife. Quite a lot of forest went with it, and this included a river with plenty of crayfish.

The croft belonged to a farm which was owned by a relative of ours. Like other farmers in the locality, he wasn't the least bit interested in crayfishing. As far as he was concerned, the timber was the only thing worth having about Stacka. So he had no objections to us going crayfishing twice every autumn.

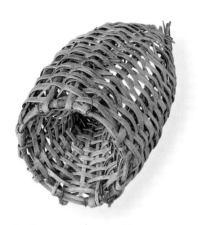

Superbly and durably crafted crayfishing gear. The oblong trap was made in Småland in the 1920s. The square one, from Västergötland is over a century old.

Preparations

Preparations for the crayfishing occupied two days. Bag nets, traps and cages had to be got out and overhauled, netting was carefully checked and mended, lines were tested and if necessary replaced. Then there was bait to be got. An acquaintance of ours was a keen fisherman and sometimes went crayfishing with us. He would put some fish by for us in a corf; roach and bullhead were considered best. There was other equipment to be overhauled as well: paraffin lamps and primus stove, rubber boots, rainwear just in case, and last but not least, an adequate supply of mosquito repellant.

The coloured float indicates who owns the trap.

There was work for my mother as well. Pickled herring, fried meatballs, mushroom omelette, bread and cheese and lots more besides had to be got ready. An old enamel coffee pot was pressed back into service, together with saucepans, china, cutlery, serving dishes, cloths and blankets. As the finishing touch, there was dill to be picked and beer and lemonade to be shopped. On crayfishing expeditions we children were allowed an unlimited supply of lemonade, a privilege otherwise reserved for birthdays.

The journey

So at last the great afternoon came round. The other families taking part arrived noisily, mostly with one or two children of my own age whom I knew already. The cars were loaded up, and off we went, with our car taking the lead. It was only about 10 km to Stacka, but the journey seemed endless. I was impatient, of cour-

Fishing for crayfish in Småland during the 1950s. The cages are baited with perch and lowered into the water with purpose-cut poles. Before the first collecting round begins, there is time for a picnic.
(Photographs privately owned.)

se, but the last mile or so through the woods was almost impassable. As we ground along in first gear, the fragrance of our provisions mingled with the odour of crayfish traps and leaky paraffin lamps. When we parked at the croft, we still had a kilometre to walk through the forest down to the river, trudging along like overloaded pack mules.

Division of labour

On arrival we got down to business with great urgency, following a division of labour which was never discussed or challenged. The mothers spread out blankets and cloths and pumped the primus stove for the first round of coffee, while the fathers got out the fish and began baiting the traps and cages. One fish gave three or four baits. It had to be cut carefully, so that the innards would be included in each piece, making the smell as strong as possible. This was quite a messy job, performed on the scale-glittering newspaper which the fish had been wrapped in. Then, shouldering our gear, we began setting up the traps under the river bank.

The long wait

When all the traps had been set it was time for coffee (with a nip of something stronger for the grown-ups) and a bit of a rest. Darkness gradually descended and the excitement rose, with everyone chatting and laughing and trying to predict the year's catch. Had the summer been too dry or hot? Had the crayfish had time to

change shells properly, so that they would not turn soft and pale red when boiled? Had someone got there ahead of us and been poaching? – Wasn't the grass looking a bit flat in some places along the bank? There was a heavy fragrance of daphne, wormwood and river water, the wind whispered in the tall pine trees and the moon rose slowly above the black edge of the forest.

The catch

At about half past eight, before it was too dark, the time had finally come for the first inspection of the traps.

 We marched in single file – fathers first, children last. The mothers mostly stayed behind to boil the dill and water and get things ready for the real crayfish party later. The traps were emptied one by one to what was almost a ritual commentary: "There's a tough old brute for you," or "This one's been in the wars and lost a claw," or "That poor little blighter'll keep until next year – throw him back."

Illegally by torchlight

After the proud trappers had returned, proclaimed their exploits to the mums and refreshed themselves, fishing was resumed, this time with torches. This was prohibited, which made it all the more exciting. There was one point in the river where the current was a bit faster, the bed was stony and the water only three of four decimetres deep – just the place for lighting up the river bed without

Darkness has descended but sound and smells betray the presence of good company and fresh-cooked crayfish. A wonderful memory!

getting water in your boots (except now and again). For us nippers especially, it was a thrilling experience, cautiously lifting the stones, pointing the torch and quickly stretching out a hand to grab a crayfish.

The party

By the time we got back to the camp it was almost pitch dark, but the lanterns were already ready visible between the trees from a long way off. People were laughing and talking and in a real party mood, and the natural fragrance of the forest was drowned by that of fresh-cooked crayfish and other good things. We sat in a big circle round the assembled delicacies, among which of course the crayfish had pride of place. Although – this being a test run – we didn't need so many, they were delicious, even though they had not yet cooled properly in their liquor and in spite of us having neither paper moons, bibs or funny hats.

Somehow those accessories didn't belong in the forest. Sometimes Herman and Ameli, the old crofter couple, would join us in this banquet in the bosom of nature. I hardly think

they ate any crayfish — if they did, it would be out of politeness — but they greatly enjoyed all the other food and drink. Happy as they were in our uncomplicated company, they definitely thought we were rather odd, dragging a load of food into the forest and sitting there, eating and making a big noise, in the middle of the night. The forest, the river and the darkness were not, in their minds, associated with food or pastime and good company.

There are more ways than one of catching crayfish, but only one kind of welcome for them!

The return

The party ended towards midnight. By now the mist would be rising over the river and there was a chill in the air. All our clutter had to be put back into the bags and baskets, the traps had to be retrieved and emptied and everything carried back to the cars.

Hardly any Swedish artists have left such an imprint on the minds of the Swedish people as Carl Larsson (1853-1919), with his realistic, highly detailed depictions of his home, family life and people round about him. The highlights of the seasons and festivals of the year are lovingly recorded and interiors and fashions reproduced in a manner which remains influential today.

The pictures emanating from the artist's home at Sundborn, in the Central Swedish province of Dalarna (Dalekarlia), epitomise what many regard as a quintessentially Swedish way of life – in which, of course, the national crayfish tradition has its appointed place.

If the truth be known, the crayfish of Sundborn had been artificially introduced. The big cauldron and the fishing in progress make one wonder if the old habit of eating the crayfish warm still lived on in Dalarna at this time. What wouldn't one give to be joining them!

Editorial note: Following the depredations of "crayfish plague", new stocks – this time of Signal Crayfish – have been introduced at Sundborn.

Björn Halling

How I cook them

There are just about as many "best crayfish liquors" as there are cooks, but I would still like to pass on a few hints which have helped me over the years and whose results have been widely appreciated.

Crayfish are caught and cooked live, and the law actually prohibits the preparation of those which have died naturally. You are not even allowed to return dead crayfish to your supplier, if you obtained them commercially, so it is your responsibility to make sure that any dead crayfish are destroyed and never used for human consumption.

Cooking

The first thing to do is to rinse the live crayfish carefully, partly to ensure that none of the bait gets into the cooking pot. Otherwise the effects on flavour are disastrous.

How much liquor

After putting the crayfish in water for rinsing, add just enough freshwater to cover them **in the pan they are going to be cooked in**. Drain off and measure the water and use the same quantity for cooking.

Killing

Take a big saucepan and fill it 3/4 full with pure, unsalted water. Put it on full heat and wait until it boils vigorously.

Now take a small number of crayfish at a time and kill them in the boiling water. Rule of thumb: 6 crayfish at a time in a 2-litre saucepan 3/4 full of bubbling water. Allow just over a minute to kill the crayfish.

N.B. The old habit of putting all the crayfish into the liquor at once on an ordinary kitchen cooker can be terri-

bly cruel. With more than about a kilo of crayfish, the cooker will not be powerful enough to counteract the cooling effect of the crayfish. So give them a swift, clean death by bringing the water to the boil before putting the next batch into it.

Live crayfish in a coarse-meshed metal basket are lowered into the boiling water and taken out again after just over a minute – a quick and easy method.

The liquor

After all the crayfish have been killed, the liquor is prepared. This has to boil for 15 minutes before the crayfish are put into it. The crayfish then have to boil for 6 or 7 minutes.

You have already worked out the amount of liquor needed during the rinsing process.

Ingredients:

3 l. water
2 dl coarse Mediterranean salt
2 lumps of sugar
0.5 l. lightly pressed dill crowns (boiling liquor)
0.5 l. lightly pressed dill crowns (after-liquor)
1 bottle of porter/stout
1 small onion

The onion gives a fuller flavour, but it is not advisable if the crayfish are to be stored cold for more than two days, because the liquor may then go off.

Note that two lots of dill are needed, because after cooking the crayfish have to be placed on new, fresh dill crowns in the cooling and storage vessel. Don't use complete stems, because that will mean too many thick stalks, which do not really add to the flavour and only take up room.

First strain the boiling liquor over the new dill crowns, then put in the crayfish and cool as quickly as possible. Make sure the liquor covers the crayfish, and leave to stand for 24 hours.

Serving

The ideal dish for crayfish is bowl-shaped, but still wide, so that a certain amount of liquor can also be included.

Many people enjoy dipping the crayfish into the liquor several times and having a good slurp. For garnish, use fresh dill crowns if possible, but the ones in the liquor will do at a pinch.

One old custom is to arrange the crayfish neatly with the "face" and claws outwards and the backs upwards. The biggest and finest are usually reserved and put on top of the mound, not only for the sake of appearances but so that they can be offered first to the guest of honour or favourite lady.

Main picture, page 58.
The dill bouquet ought really to include tender flowers and hard seedpods, which together create an aroma vastly superior to that of shortcuts using dill seeds and dill oil.

Robert Bergquist

Drinks and punch

A fresh, tasty drink before the meal greatly improves the prospects of the party being a success. The senses of taste and smell are started up and the appetite pleasurably teased.

But we don't want to deaden the taste buds before the first course is even served. Somebody who has been working body and soul in the kitchen may well feel slighted if full justice cannot be done to the food. This ought to rule out strong spirits as an aperitif. A glass of cognac or armagnac, whisky or calvados has its appointed place, but mainly after the meal and normally together with good coffee.

Something weaker, then, will make a better upbeat. Most white wines, sparkling ones not least, are good appetisers. Wine can also form the basis of a personal, tasty punch.

Dry or medium-dry wines are very commonly used as aperitifs, but sweeter ones are also good, especially perhaps during the darker season of the year.

In addition there are a large number of special aperitif wines to choose from, ranging from dry to sweet and with various flavours and seasonings. The rule here is: do your own thing. Many of these wines mix well with soda water or can be served on the rocks.

If you don't mind forking out for a well-made, dry champagne, this is a perfect beginning.

On the other hand, those who have come to appreciate a dry sherry seldom look round for alternatives, least of all in summertime. The following are some plain but dependable recipes, with one or two hints thrown in, to guarantee a good start to your crayfish party. The main picture shows, from left to right, the following drinks.

Barry's bubbly

Fix a sprig of peppermint or a few leaves of lemon balm and a maraschino cherry which is then let down carefully into a glass full of dry, sparkling wine.

Heart's delight

A glass of dry, fresh sparkling wine is topped with a dessert spoon of lemon sorbet. Garnish with a few small, brittle leaves of lemon balm.

Raspberry surprise

There is always a special kick to be got out of using fruit and berries of your own gathering. For this recipe, summer raspberries from the freezer add extra colour and flavour.

Sugar the edge of the glass with raspberry liqueur and sugar. Carefully pour a few cl of the liqueur into the glass and then top up with dry sparkling wine. Garnish with a few frozen raspberries.

Champagne

Sir Winston Churchill, a great lover of champagne, is supposed to have said that it should always be dry, cold and free.

I fully agree about the dryness and mode of supply, but on the other hand I think champagne is often served too cold, sometimes even ice cold. A dry standard champagne is best served at 9 or 10 degrees, and superior qualities of mature vintage character should be served a little warmer still.

Remember that the champagne glass is the only one you fill right to the top — to about 1.5 cm from the rim.

Punch – easy to make, good to drink and ideal for self-service!

Dry sherry

A glass of cool, dry sherry (Manzanilla or Fino) makes a perfect apéritif, especially together with slightly bolder, tasty snacks as the prelude to something so personal and tasty as the traditional Swedish crayfish.

Cucumber and lemon punch

A fresh, appetising drink made with 75 cl dry, white, fruity wine, half a bottle of sparkling wine, half a well-washed lemon in thin slices and strips of cucumber.

For a portrait of Robert Bergquist, see p. 71.

Björn Halling

Snacks

A good drink before the meal can very well be combined with something more adventurous than two bags of crisps or peanuts. A bit more effort pays dividends in terms of the guests' appreciation and your own self-esteem.

There's nothing difficult or time-consuming about making good, interesting appetisers to go with the drink and give the party a flying start. Added to which, they make a tasteful, moderately filling introduction to the evening's menu.

The following is a selection of appetisers, some traditional and some less common, using both everyday and more expensive ingredients.

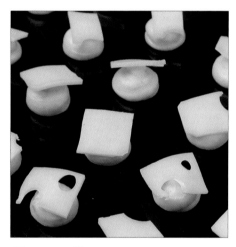

Cheese puffs
The hollow, feather-light cheese puff goes with most wines and with all the drinks we have suggested.

Ingredients:
1 dl water
50 g butter
60 g flour
2 eggs
100 g Gruyère or Finnish Emmenthaler cheese

Procedure:
1. Heat the water and butter on a slow

flame. Stir in the flour with a wooden spoon until you get a supple "dumpling" which does not stick to the saucepan. Transfer the hot dough to a food processor and blend in the eggs, one at a time.

2. Use a forcing bag to squirt walnut-sized balls onto a greased baking sheet, not too close together. Put a slice of cheese on each ball and bake at 275° for 10-12 minutes.

Tapenade

Ingredients:
350 g black olives (kalamata)
4 cloves of garlic
5 sprigs of parsley (without the stalks)
2 cl Armagnac

100 g anchovy fillets
0.5 dl olive oil
juice of half a lemon

Procedure:
1. Soak the anchovy fillets in Vichy water for 10 minutes.

2. Pit the olives. Blend olives, garlic, parsley and Armagnac in a food processor.

3. Salt to taste with the anchovy fillets. Flavour with olive oil and lemon.

Ideal on a slice of home-made farm bread and with a glass of dry Fino sherry.

Potted cheese
This remarkable mixture varies a great deal in flavour, depending on the cheese and seasoning used. It is a good way of using up odds and ends of cheese. In Sweden it belongs to starter cheeses and the herring table. We serve it with a moderately bitter dark beer, such as Altbier, which is also an optional drink with the crayfish.

Ingredients:
Oddments of different cheeses, with rind and dry edges carefully removed.
Soft butter

Seasoning:
Caraway and/or paprika powder
Cognac or flavoured schnapps
Cayenne pepper

Procedure:
1. Grate or grind the cheese finely. Blend with the butter into a firm mixture; the amount of butter will depend on the types of cheeses.

2. Season boldly with caraway and/or paprika and cognac or schnapps. Add more salt if necessary and don't be too mean with the cayenne pepper.

3. Blend the mixture and herbs thoroughly, season to taste and transfer to a china pot. Keep the potted cheese under plastic foil, serve it from the pot.

Grapes rolled in pistachios

Ingredients:
100 g processed cheese
200 g Roquefort cheese
1 kg green grapes
300 g pistachio nuts (peeled)

1. Make a smooth blend of the processed cheese and Roquefort in a food processor. The processed cheese provides an adhesive coating for the grapes.

2. Pick the grapes – juicy ones! – from the bunch and blend them carefully with the cheese mixture.

3. Chop the pistachios (by all means in the food processor) into 2-3 mm pieces.

4. Retrieve the grapes one by one and roll them in the chopped pistachios. Put the grapes in paper cases for petits fours. An excellent snack with dry white vermouth, or a white apéritif wine like Lillet.

Mini-croustards with cottage cheese filling

Ingredients:
5 tufts of dill
1 tub of cottage cheese
salt, pepper
1 packet of mini-croustards

Procedure:
Chop the dill tops finely. Mix with cottage cheese, salt and pepper. Squirt into the mini-croustards and garnish with a tuft of dill each.

Goes well with a dry, white wine with a fresh, grapy flavour, such as a Sauvignon Blanc.

Suggested canapés for our drinks

1. Tapenade with lemon.
2. Grevé cheese with red paprika and black olives.
3. Potted cheese with red paprika and parsley.
4. Slice of avocado, tomato, walnut and leek.
5. Wafer-thin slice of lime, trout's roe, crème fraiche.
6. Russian caviar, crème fraiche.

When planning the crayfish party, we say, without really thinking about it, that we must have a drink and a few snacks. Why not make the drink and the snacks part of the overall plan? If there are many guests, they may take a long time to gather. So make the drink uncomplicated and easy to replenish.

If you are not serving a starter, the snacks with the drinks can be made a little more substantial – a moderately filling introduction to the meal.

And don't forget to have non-alcoholic alternatives available right from the start.

Ready, steady...

A stimulating drink and a tasteful appetiser have done their part, the taste buds are wide open and our nostrils are keeping us firmly on course.

No matter whether the table is laid with beautifully patterned china and glittering cut glass, or with plainer disposable articles – more fun tomorrow morning! – the crayfish and their accessories are the centre of attention.

Crayfish are piled high on the turned-up dishes, and their tasty liquor can be glimpsed and scented. Crowns of dill provide the finishing touch. A generous cheese board promises many gustatory delights. White toast, butter and cheese make every mouthful a delicacy. Crisp bread is ready to hand, offering a further sensation with one of the other cheeses. The schnapps glasses promise familiar sensations but also arouse expectations of surprises – patent, secret flavourings.

The thought of the saltness of the crayfish, much singing and lively conversation sends one's gaze in quest of big glasses of foaming beer.

Attractive options are provided for those who prefer weaker drinks. When the eye and the nose are sated, it only remains to settle down to that most Swedish of institutions – a genuine crayfish party.

But hold on a minute!

Perhaps the spectacle of these delights will prompt one or two practical considerations. Guests who, sadly, are allergic to shellfish can perhaps be offered a warm crown artichoke. The swift disappearance of the crayfish can be forestalled with a thick chanterelle soup for starters. Those who have room for more after eating their fill can be given a dessert and gâteau with their coffee.

No need to go hungry from the table!

Björn Halling
A starter all the same?

Chanterelle soup

Although crayfish in every way are the principal meal of the evening and do not really need the backing of an extensive menu, a small starter may not be out of place.

Delicious as they are, crayfish don't have much meat on them, and one or two people may still be hungry when the dishes are empty. A substantial starter is one way of avoiding this risk. Mushroom soup is just the thing, especially when made from fresh chanterelles. The following version is made extra full-bodied by adding half the chanterelles at the last minute.

Ingredients (serves 4-6):
1 l. chanterelles
1 piece of celeriac
1 shallot
1 tbsp butter
1 tsp flour
1 l. stock (cube will do)
1 dl double cream

Procedure:
1. Clean the mushrooms and put the best-looking half to one side.

2. Clean the vegetables, chop them and the mushrooms and heat in half the butter.

3. Dust with the flour and add the stock. Cook for 15 minutes.

4. Heat the remaining chanterelles in the rest of the butter.

5. Run the soup in the food processor, season to taste. Return to the heat and add the cream.

6. Serve, garnished with the second batch of mushrooms.

To drink? Robert's advice:
Very often it seems rather unnecessary, serving a drink with the soup, which after all is liquid any way. Traditional drinks with soup are dry to medium-dry Madeira and dry Oloroso sherry or suchlike. Given the apricot-like aroma of the chanterelles and the creamy texture of the soup, a tasty Riesling with a

Soup of fresh chanterelles? The crayfish can wait for a bit!

good balance between acidity and sweetness is well worth testing.

Choose a Kabinett or Spätlese quality from Rheinpfalz, Rheingau or Baden. Remember to serve cooled, not ice-cold.

Björn Halling

Instead of crayfish

Crown artichoke

There can be many reasons for wanting to serve something else as well as crayfish. Somebody may not like crayfish – incredible! – and some unfortunates are allergic to them. We suggest that, for their comfort, you give them a well-made, warm crown artichoke.

Undeniably, the crown artichoke has a certain amount in common with the crayfish. You take it apart, leaf by leaf, and suck out the meaty parts with a little butter until, finally, you have exposed the delicate base – rather like the delicious tails of the crayfish. Not a bad substitute, is it?

The art of dressing a crown artichoke

1. Grasp the long stalk at the bottom of the crown artichoke and snap it off.
2. The stalk will then take the coarse fibres with it.
3. Cut away the short leaves at the bottom.
4. Cut off the tips of the outer leaves with a pair of scissors and remove the very top with a knife. This reduces the bulk and makes the artichoke look tidier.
5. Rub the bottom part of the artichoke with a slice of lemon which you then tie in position. The bleaching effect of the lemon offsets the oxidisation (dark-staining) caused by boiling.

WARNING! Handling the artichoke leaves a bitter flavour on your hands, so before handling any other foodstuffs, rub your hands with a slice of lemon and wash up.

Procedure:

Cook the crown artichokes in lightly salted water for about 25 minutes. They can be packed close together.

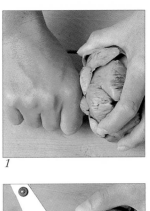

1

2

3

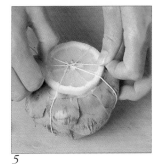

4

5

Differently served

Cheese!

White toast, crisp bread, butter and cheese are a traditional accompaniment of crayfish.

Two indispensable classics of the modern crayfish party – Västerbotten cheese and a matured *Prästost* – date from the end of the 19th century.

Some people may prefer a strong herb-flavoured cheese, e.g. one flavoured with caraway.

No matter whether the crayfish are the main course or a starter, one or two cheeses will be quite enough. But if you want a wider repertoire we recommend *Herrgårdsost, Grevé* or why not a home-made potted cheese? For a more exotic touch, we suggest an Emmenthaler, either from its native Switzerland or from Finland, which has several fine versions of its own.

The advantage of serving cheese with crayfish, of course, is that it makes a fine aromatic contribution of its own and at the same time goes well with the delicate, distinctive flavour of the crayfish.

Relishing a cold Swedish crayfish, boiled in dill, with a slice of Västerbotten cheese and with the full moon beaming down on the company, you can almost hear the whisper of the birch trees and the sounds of an accordion across a shining, motionless expanse of water – an authentically Swedish culinary sensation.

The party has begun and an anxious guest keeps a jealous watch on his plate while the photographer hovers over it. He has only had time for one bite and has barely touched the cheese – Riddarkryddost, incidently.

Cheese is a very ancient ingredient of Swedish diet. Well-preserved cheese-making equipment has been found in peat bogs, which gives cheese a history going back to the Stone Age. The real take-off came in monastic times, during the 16th century, and with the industrialisation of dairy production at the end of the 19th century, cheese factories sprang up in almost every village of Sweden.

1. Kryddsvecia
2. Svecia
3. Herrgård
4. Kryddsvecia
5. Wästgöta Kloster
6. Prästost
7. Herrgård
8. Kryddost
9. Riddarkrydd
10. Falkenberger
11. Kvibille Special
12. Grevé

Robert Bergquist

Schnapps, beer and other drinks

Schnapps – history in brief

Schnapps first came to Sweden at the beginning of the 15th century, when it was marketed by Lübeck merchants – for making gunpowder!

At about the same time, the Swedes were introduced to the gentle art of distilling by foreign mercenaries.

Almost a hundred years later, during King Johan III's Russian campaign in 1572, the Swedish troops had their first taste of Russian schnapps, distilled from grain.

The practice of distilling schnapps now spread rapidly, first – as usual – in the upper reaches of society, but soon enough to towns and big villages and, eventually, to people's homes.

All through the 17th century, distilling was an integral, and legal, part of the domestic economy. Then it was intermittently prohibited and derestricted, but the present-day ban has been in force since 1885.

On the other hand it has always been legal to flavour one's own, legally purchased schnapps. Home-flavoured schnapps has a history which is long, variegated and tasty.

The two plain varieties of schnapps – Kron Vodka and Sundsvalls Taffel – in the middle of our big picture are ideal for home-flavouring.

These and other unflavoured brands can also be seen on crayfish tables, but our aim is to make a very special culinary experience out of the crayfish and what is drunk with them. It is the combination of a personally, carefully flavoured schnapps and home-cooked crayfish that gives the whole party its special atmosphere of a culinary experience out of the ordinary.

The other brands in the picture – Bäska droppar, Snälleröds Besk, Strand Bäsq, Absolut Citron, Ödåkra Taffel Aquavit, O.P. Anderson and Gammal Norrlands Akvavit – are described further on in this chapter.

Perhaps it was the heavy lifting in liquor stores at the time which helped Robert Bergquist to get his job interview with Systembolaget, Sweden's alcohol monopoly. In student days he had been a part-time stevedore.

Today Robert is one of Systembolaget's five product advisors and a pioneer of his profession. He is much in demand, within Systembolaget and elsewhere, as a lecturer and tutor. His thorough training has been acquired in Sweden, Germany (the German Wine Academy at Kloster Eberbach) and France (Ecole du Vin at Château Loudenne), and of course he knows just about all there is to know about Systembolaget's ample product range. He is also widely informed about food, which makes him just the man to advise on appropriate drinks for a good meal of any kind, the Swedish crayfish party included.

All the drink recommendations in this book are Robert Bergquist's.

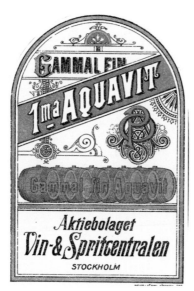

Labels from the Historical Museum of Wines and Spirits, Stockholm.

Men of good cheer

Of the four flavoured brands of schnapps among the oldest in Systembolaget's product range, two come from military gentlemen, one from a shipowner and schnapps distiller and the fourth from a wholesale merchant.

We have Major General Carl Ulric Kuylenstjerna to thank for Nyköpings Brännvin. For a long time his special mixture, using caraway, aniseed and sugar, was known as General Kuylenstjerna's mixture, and it rose to fame at the 1866 Stockholm Exhibition. In 1927 it was taken over by the liquor monopoly and renamed Nyköpings Brännvin, but with its old name as a sub-heading until 1933.

Count Colonel Hugo Jacob Hamilton was another schnapps connoisseur. As commanding officer of the King's Own Hussars (1881-1893), he handed his recipe to the Örebro Distilling Company, which accordingly supplied him with "The Colonel's Schnapps". Eventually the recipe passed into the hands of the national monopoly, and in 1921 it was renamed Äkta Örebro Överste Brännvin ("Genuine Örebro Colonel Schnapps").

The O.P. Anderson brand of schnapps was originally called O.P. Aquavit and first appeared at the 1891 Göteborg Exhibition. Its author, Olof Peter Anderson, did not achieve his present honourable mention until the recipe was taken over by the national monopoly.

Spiced schnapps…

The habit of spicing and flavouring schnapps dates from the time when the distilled product was often impure and fusel and other substances gave it a nasty taste.

So herbs and spices were mainly added as a cover-up. Physicians made much use of spiced and flavoured brännvin, in this way contributing to further developments.

The "schnapps table" became a standard feature of country and middle-class homes in the 18th century. The men would gather round it before the main meal to sharpen their appetites with herring, bread and butter and schnapps.

In the following century, railways were built, together with inns and restaurants where passengers could help themselves to a meal from what had now become the smörgåsbord. Spiced schnapps had its appointed place here, and there were many different flavours to choose from.

Many of the spiced brands of schnapps on sale today were introduced in the second half of the 19th century, so that some recipes are over a century old – Nyköpings Brännvin (1866), O.P. Anderson (1891), Överste Brännvin (1893) and Ödåkra Taffel Aquavit (1899), to mention but a few.

…for the taste

When choosing schnapps for a meal, one goes of course by the same principles as for other mealtime drinks, the aim being to provide as pleasant a culinary sensation as possible. The aroma

Our schnapps brands have stayed with us for centuries, but drinking vessels have moved on a bit – from these wooden primitives on the left to the Orrefors beauties on the right.

and taste of the spiced schnapps must, at best, harmonise with the components of the food, so that the two will either reinforce one another or create new taste sensations.

Spiced schnapps for the sake of the crayfish

Personally, I drink a spiced schnapps with my food – crayfish in this case, for the taste of it. To do justice to one's favourite flavouring, the schnapps ought to be served cool, 14-16 degrees, but never straight from the fridge. To give the schnapps a chance of doing itself justice, one should never knock it all back at once. Give your taste buds and nostrils a chance of relishing the flavouring – stomachs, after all, have no sense of taste or smell!

Use your own flavouring

The flavour of schnapps you prefer for the traditional Swedish crayfish party depends, of course, on your own preference.

Personal flavourings are fun for the host to offer and a welcome change and surprise to the guests.

The brands which I am now going to present are a supremely personal selection, but I hope that some guidance and inspiration can be had from it.

Joh. Isak Nelson, a wholesale merchant, built a distillery in Ödåkra, Skåne, just before the turn of the century. The product range included a number of schnapps varieties, and the label for Ödåkra Taffel Aquavit was registered in 1899. Is there a hidden connection here? Between the two officers' interest in schnapps and its role in the production of gunpowder? Between the manufacturer's and the merchant's interest in distilling and the increasing popularity in their circles of eating crayfish the way we do? For many people prefer O.P. and Ödåkra to Överste and – perhaps more so – Nyköpings with their crayfish.

A word of warning
An ice-cold dram of unflavoured schnapps is, more than anything else, a survival test, and the possible physical reactions to it can hardly be termed positive taste sensations. Drinking excessively cold schnapps, for example chilled outdoors on a really frosty winter's day, can damage your health. Schnapps containing 40 per cent alcohol only freezes at $-23.5°$ and well, above that, is nothing for sensitive mucous membranes. Though that shouldn't be too much of a risk at a crayfish party!

Don't forget the serving temperature for the flavoured schnapps. Cool, 14-16°. Never straight from the fridge.

Schnapps recipes

Skabbenäs dill schnapps

This recipe calls for advance planning because, to get the best out of it, the schnapps has to be kept in a cool, dark place for a year. Pick out your best, ripe dill crowns for the flavour, plus – for colour – one or two crowns which are still in bloom. Put them all into a close-fitting litre bottle. Fill this with unflavoured schnapps and cork it. Leave on the window ledge for a few weeks. Strain through a cloth and put the schnapps to mature, preferably for a whole year. Dilute to taste, roughly 1/10 dill schnapps and 9/10 unflavoured.

Rosehip schnapps

A mild, finely coloured schnapps for those who don't get on very well with flavoured varieties.

From a full bottle of plain schnapps, pour about 15 cl into a suitable vessel. Add ripe rosehips, few enough for the schnapps to cover them. Cover and leave for a fortnight. Strain through a cloth and reserve the essence in the bottle. Allow at least a fortnight to mature.

Wormwood schnapps – bitter

Bitter schnapps is the kingpin of the Skåne schnapps tradition – allegedly the secret of good health among the fishing population of the south coast. Both they and the local farmers took a dram every morning.

There are presumably as many recipes for bitter schnapps as there are lovers of it, but here are two procedures to choose from.

Mulled bitter schnapps

Put a teaspoonful of newly picked flower buds on a dish. Pour on schnapps to cover. Ignite and reduce the liquid by half (easier if you heat the dish first). Strain off the flowers. Repeat until you have the amount you need for making your bitter. Dilute to taste. This gives you a slightly gentler, aromatic bitter schnapps.

Bitter

For a more herbal character, take a full bottle of plain schnapps and pour 6-7 cl into a coffee cup. Top up with newly gathered wormwood flowers and cover with plastic film. Leave for a fortnight. Strain carefully and leave for a bit while the sediment settles. Pour off the clear essence, decant and pour about 4 cl back into the bottle of plain schnapps. Leave to mature for at least a fortnight. Wormwood blooms from June to September, and the morning of St. Bartholomew's day is considered the best time for harvesting.

Lemon schnapps

Peel a carefully washed lemon thinly, so that none of the white pith is included. Put the peel into a full bottle of plain schnapps. Leave for about a week and flavour to taste. If the flavour is too weak, leave for another day or so. If it is too strong, add a little more schnapps.

A fresh, pleasant-tasting schnapps that goes well with crayfish.

Blackberry schnapps

A schnapps with a beautiful colour and a well-rounded aroma of berries which can be an alternative for those usually preferring blackberry schnapps.

Empty half of a full bottle of plain schnapps into a suitable vessel. Add ripe blackberries until they are just covered by the schnapps. Leave to stand for a few weeks. Strain the essence and leave to stand for a few weeks again. Decant. Return the essence to the bottle and store for a few weeks. Done!

Tansy schnapps

Tansy in Sweden blooms between July and September, and it's the flowers you want. This is a strong-smelling plant and no large quantities are needed. It gives the schnapps a pure, distinct flavour which is just the thing with shellfish.

Take a full bottle of plain schnapps and pour 5 cl into a cup. Add flowers for the schnapps to cover. Cover over with plastic film and leave for just under a week. Strain off the flowers and return the essence to the bottle.

This recipe also works with yarrow (milfoil), but in that case the flowers must be left in the schnapps for one or two weeks, to extract the flavour and colour.

Corresponding Systembolaget brands

Systembolaget's range of flavoured schnapps includes three wormwood brands and one lemon-flavoured.

Bäska droppar is robustly bitter in character and has little in common with the two woodworm recipes described here.

Snälleröds Besk has a mild, rounded, aromatic wormwood aroma with a touch of sweetness in the after-taste. Suitable perhaps for those drinking bitter schnapps for the first time or preferring a mild variety.

Strand Bäsq has a delicate, aromatic fragrance and tastes of wormwood.

Absolut Citron has a pure, fresh aroma and a citrus flavour with a slightly dry, distinct after-taste.

Other herbs commonly used for flavouring schnapps are coriander, caraway and fennel, and there are numerous brands of schnapps based on various recipes, most of them genuine classics.

Specially worth mentioning are *Ödåkra Taffel Aquavit*, with its strong, dry taste of caraway, *O.P. Anderson* with its richly composite flavouring, and *Gammal Norrlands Akvavit*, which is distinctly flavoured with fennel, coriander and a dash of sherry.

Pale or dark ale with the crayfish?

When I serve beer with crayfish, I usually give people a few different kinds to choose from. There are many different flavours and fragrances to be had. Personally I prefer a top-fermented, slightly darker beer like an English ale, a German *Altbier* or Swedish Carnegie Pale Ale with its exciting, slightly roasted aroma, which goes very well with salty flavours, the aroma of dill and the taste of crayfish. Slightly darker beer goes very well indeed, for example, with a caraway or Västerbotten cheese. This sort of beer has to be served cool – 14 or 16 degrees, but preferably no colder.

For a drink which is also more thirst-quenching, I recommend a pale lager or pilsner. The hopping rate is a matter of taste, and there are any number of brands to choose from. These kinds of beer can very well be served a bit colder, 10-12 degrees.

Schnapps and beer – not everyone's poison

Many people, of course, take the view that, at a Swedish crayfish party, there should be beer and schnapps to drink and nothing else. Of course, traditions of food and drink are not to be trifled with and there is much to be said for preserving them as part of our cultural heritage.

But there is no harm in listening to present-day arguments about food and drink, and hospitality demands allowance for each guest's right to choose something in keeping with his or her personal taste or preference.

A small selection from Systembolaget's collection of beer labels – from the day when "pilsner" was a commoner word for beer.

Picture page 76
The beers in the top row are lagers (bottom-fermented beers) like Åbro Original, Falcon Original (medium bitter flavour) and Pilsener Urquell (very bitter).
In the bottom row we have top-fermented beers like Carnegie Pale Ale, Diebels Alt and Samuel Smith's Pale Ale.

Wine...

Those who can do without beer and schnapps but enjoy a glass of white wine on other occasions can do the same with crayfish. But if wine is to be served, one has to think still more carefully about the saltness of the crayfish.

Avoid the driest of white wines and instead go for one which is grapy and aromatic, with a touch of residual sweetness. Very often, an aromatic, medium-dry wine with a good, pure grape taste will do fine. Avoid wines matured in the wood!

Remember that wine should be served at 10-12 degrees. If the bottles are put out with no cooler, they will soon get too warm.

A dry cider makes an exciting drink with crayfish, but perhaps not as a first-time experience: that introduction ought preferably to come with some other kind of food.

...or non-alcoholic

There is plenty of scope today for those not wishing to serve any alcohol at all or requiring a non-alcoholic alternative. Table beer ("light beer") is the obvious choice, but there are also a number of very good non-alcoholic beers to choose from.

There is non-alcoholic cider as well, but be sure to get a "grown-up", drier one. This nearly always goes better with food than the sweeter, fruitier kinds.

Lastly, remember that good table water is often the best drink with a meal and should normally be included on every table.

There is a wide and tasty range of low-alcohol drinks to go with crayfish. Don't forget a refreshing table water – Ramlösa is a classic!

Christina Mattsson

A song for every claw

In articles for learned journals and a number of books, for both academic and table-side use, Christina Mattsson has made clear, once and for all, the importance attached by the Swedish people to the drinking song.

Christina is basically a folk song researcher, specialising in "toasting songs". At the end of the 70s, though, came the chance of an attractive job with the Swedish Broadcasting Corporation, where she is now Director of Channel 2.

The Whole and the Half: These expressions are descended from the schnapps table of the 18th century, where the gentlemen would start with two drams – the first brim-full, the second only half-full. The ensuing third, fourth and fifth drams came to be known as tersen, kvarten and kvinten, probably in the 19th century among students with a knowledge of Latin. The custom of only half-filling the second glass eventually disappeared, in favour of full glasses all the way. The at times rather tumultuous drinking habits of the Swedes have, over the years, necessitated further designations for an even longer succession of drams, but these, in view of their uncertain history and untranslatability, are better left aside.

The 19th century was the century of schnapps – and the century which, with the emergence of the middle class, transformed our crayfish customs. A natural link was established between the drinking of schnapps and the new ceremonies which were created, at the same time as crayfish eating became increasingly widespread.

One and a half...

Schnapps occupied a dominant position, both at the dinner-time smörgåsbord and on other occasions. For a restaurant or tavern breakfast the schnapps glass would be put out together with the knife, fork and napkin. The half-dram belonged with the whole one and cost nothing extra.

The Nordic student rallies, the flowering of the student leagues and other activities in the university towns had created a market for special student songs, cultivated by Nybom, Wennerberg, Otto Lindblad and others. The 1840s witnessed the birth, not only of Sweden's male voice choir tradition but also of a perfect environment for the Swedish drinking song to flourish in.

...third, fourth and fifth

The student volunteers in Uppsala during the 1860s, true to the custom of the times, would swallow several drams while processing round the table and singing for the whole, the half, the third

or sometime even for the fourth and fifth. Each dram had its own song to a given tune and the ranking order between them was meticulously observed.

New times, old songs

People of the middle classes gathering for crayfish parties at the beginning of the century were well-versed in all the rituals of schnapps drinking. The songs usually sung in praise of schnapps were also sung with the drams accompanying the succession of crayfish claws.

Nobody knows today how many schnapps drinking songs there are. The number seems infinite, and anyone dissatisfied with the existing repertoire can make up a new song by the simple expedient of taking an easy tune which everyone knows and composing words which will catch on easily.

Making up new words for old, familiar tunes is a proven, centuries-old practice. This has been done with songs of all kinds, but seldom as distinctly as with the modern schnapps drinking song, which is almost invariably sung to a previously known tune.

In this way newly composed schnapps ditties can be quickly assimilated by tradition, because everyone knows the tunes already and can concentrate on the words. And yet the amazing thing is that nine out of every ten new ditties nowadays employ tunes between 75 and 100 years old.

Johan Nybom: 1817-1864, poet with a penchant for high-flown student songs and tear-drenched bathos.
Gunnar Wennerberg: 1817-1901, poet and composer but also Sweden's Minister for Ecclesiastical Affairs, in 1870-75.
Otto Lindblad: 1809-1864, composer and founder of the Lund University Chorus.

Wennerberg and Lindblad wrote some of the best-known songs in the Swedish vocal tradition.

Tersen, kvarten and kvinten: For an explanation, see The Whole and The Half, above.

Helan går: A classical Swedish schnapps ditty, reproduced and further explained below under the heading *To sing or not to sing*.

Translation of the schnapps ditty above.

Briskly

If you think like me, then "Clink!" say we, the
dram it makes us glad and free. We take
one, we take two, we take three, four and five, and
then once again – one, two, three alive.
Moonshine up and crayfish down, fill your glass and go to town. For
– strike a light! – when I get tight, I'm good as gold – Night, night!

The notation above refers to the Swedish words but, with a little modification, will also fit the English.

Another advantage, of course, is that notation is hardly necessary. (Most people can't read music, anyway.)

The tunes may be familiar, but the authors, as a rule, are not. Virtually all schnapps ditties are anonymous, and of course the revellers, braying away to their hearts' content, couldn't care less who wrote them anyway. The subject is ready and waiting – the dram's progress from glass to throat to stomach. Season to taste with *double entendres* and a touch of insanity, and a song is born.

New habits, new songs

But crayfish do not only call for schnapps drinking songs, they need songs of their own as well. Since they have not been the common man's delicacy all that long, songs about them are a fairly new genre. In fact, it is only during our own century, with crayfish eating becoming more widespread, that the real crayfish songs have come into being.

Song researchers with a zest for recording and classification make crayfish songs a subdivision of the modern schnapps drinking song. For the characteristics are the same – the words are simple and the songs have to be sung to popular tunes which everybody knows. The melodic ideas have been taken from a widely familiar repertoire – from songs for male voice choir, nursery rhymes, school songs and current hits. More and more new songs follow in the wake of the most popular melodies, and

this is such a common practice that the tune gives the age of the song. Veiled obscenities are also regular practice, with the word "tail" working permanent overtime.

The female crayfish, consequently, is the principal character in many of these songs. Her tail is pinched, she is touched and fondled and the company have their will of her. The entertainment value of the words is enhanced by setting them to familiar singing game tunes or to tunes normally associated with more high-flown, edifying sentiments. Almost invariably, the words of the ditty are simple to the point of imbecility: the crayfish is a tasty beast, boiled bright red for a jolly good feast; if she walks backwards, she's only half-done, and if she moves forwards, then you've had a skinful.

Songs are disseminated by verbal tradition or in various printed forms. Sometimes in books of schnapps drinking songs one finds a special section for crayfish songs, but otherwise there are place-cards with crayfish songs printed on them. This is also an Eldorado of casual poetry – some songs barely deserve to be called poetry – while other creations have a life expectancy of some decades.

Crayfish songs, then, do not have a very old history, but old enough to make up a genuine, authentically Swedish tradition.

From the preface to **Sjung och drick**, drinking songs collected by Carl Möller and published by Albert Bonniers Förlag in 1933.

In these so-called hard times of ours, we are having to look for simple, inexpensive pleasures, and, happy to relate, much may come of that search, the true joy of living being, as a general rule, least expensive. Having raised the money for this book, all one need do is sing and look happy – and drink.

Drinking, of course, costs more than singing, but those who cannot afford to sing these songs with wine can sing them with beer instead – the effect is roughly the same.

The special schnapps ditties, of course, should not be profaned: they should be relished with genuine schnapps – by all means ordinary plain – otherwise they may very well evoke longing instead of satisfaction, and their purpose be frustrated. But times have never been so bad that the Swedish people have not been able to afford a dram, at least for the big festivals.

Editorial note: The above lines, then, were penned over sixty years ago, but have an obvious message for the book you are now reading. Eat, drink, sing and be happy!

To sing or not to sing?

The one internationally viable Swedish expression connected with the imbibing of schnapps or any other strong drink is **Skål!** – corresponding to the English **Cheers**!

Meaningful translation of Swedish schnapps ditties, though, is just about impossible. By far the best-known and most-sung of them is called by and opens with the words **Helan går** and, more often than not, is the kick-off for a Swedish crayfish party or for the downing of schnapps on other festive occasions. It can be more or less Englished as **Here the first (schnapps) one goes**!

Against all the odds, we have tried to give non-Swedish-speaking readers an insight into the half-baked nonsensicality of the classical schnapps ditty.

First, in numbered lines, comes the full text in Swedish, followed by a free translation and a line-by-line explanation in English.

Helan går
in swedish

1. *Helan går*
2. *sjung hopp faderallanlallan lej,*
3. *Helan går*
4. *sjung hopp faderallan lej.*
5. *Den som inte helan tar*
6. *han heller inte halvan får*
7. *Helan gåååår!*
8. *- - - - -*
9. *Sjung hoppfaderallan lej.*

1. *Here the first one goes*
Self-explanatory, we trust.

2. *Let's sing hopp faderallanlallan lej,*
Everyone's to join in, then, and for the rest of the line you just turn off your brain and give throat.

3. *Here the first one goes*
A stronger expression for line 1.

4. *Let's sing hopp faderallan lej.*
A final recapitulation of an abbreviated version of line 2.

5. *He/she who doesn't take the first one*
Conditions will now be dictated for further drinking.

6. *doesn't get a second one*
So don't miss the boat!

7. *Here the first one gooooes!*
A protracted reiteration of line 1, underscoring the importance of what you are engaged in.

8. *- - - - -*
Silence descends and drams with it – all in one go!

9. *Let's sing hopp faderallan lej.*
The ditty ends with a display of empty glasses, often accompanied by a sustained, gratified Aaaaaah!

To non-Swedish speakers, of course, the original words are quite unintelligible. The story goes, however, that an English guest, failing to understand that the company were actually singing in Swedish, tried to work out what he thought must be the original English. The result is what follows.

Helan går

as noted down by a bewildered English listener.

Hell and gore
Chunkhopp Father Allan, Lai and Lei
Hell and gore
Chunkhopp Father Allan Lei.
Oh handsome in the hell and tar
and hell ear inter hull one four –
Hell and gooooooore...
Chunkhopp Father Allan, Lei!

Occasionally, though, we go the whole hog and translate a Swedish schnapps ditty so as to make it perfectly singable in a foreign language. Here, then, is a direct English translation of an ancient Swedish tribute to Schnapps the Beloved – short, sharp and to the point.

Full idag
in english

Full to-day yesterday
and tomorrow too,
by some fullness every day
sorrow goes away.

Let's face it – the Swedes are an international people in all things, and a people with a message.

To those who have taken a fancy to the crayfish and its many culinary graces, without being fully versed in the Swedish tradition of crayfish vocalism, it may come as a reassurance to learn that crayfish go down just as well to all songs of praise, whatever the language.

Culinary anatomy of the crayfish

Unlike human beings and some other animals, the crayfish is not constructed round a skeleton. Instead all its soft tissues and organs are themselves surrounded and held together by a stout shell. One advantage of this to those of us who enjoy eating crayfish is that, once the shell has been removed from these different parts, we can eat, chew or suck at them without the risk of any bones lodging in our throats. And removing the shell is a fairly simple business.

Basically, then, the eating of crayfish is perfectly simple.

Convenience and pleasure, however, can be enhanced by a knowledge of the crayfish's culinary anatomy. Because there are certain parts which taste horrible, others which should not be missed and, finally, parts on the borderline between these two categories.

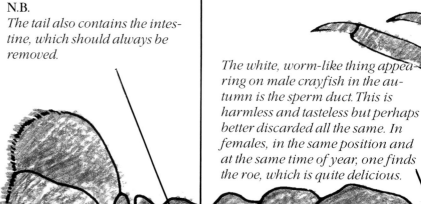

The tail, containing most of the meat, makes the whole thing worth the trouble.

N.B.
The tail also contains the intestine, which should always be removed.

The white, worm-like thing appearing on male crayfish in the autumn is the sperm duct. This is harmless and tasteless but perhaps better discarded all the same. In females, in the same position and at the same time of year, one finds the roe, which is quite delicious.

The tail fin is of no interest except as one of two measuring points – the rostrum is the other one – deciding whether the crayfish can be retained or put back into its home water. (Measurements: see opposite.)

Note *that the female has a wider tail than the male and, between October and June, carries her eggs attached to her "pleopods". The pleopods of the male are reproductive organs.*

The roe of the females can be recommended – delicious!

Inside the carapace and sometimes in the claws as well is the white butter, which is a real delicacy, not to be wasted.

N.B.
The stomach should come away with the head. Handle with some care.

The four pairs of walking legs don't contain much edible matter but are worth chewing on before putting aside.

The smaller part of the claw is often big enough to be shelled and eaten whole.

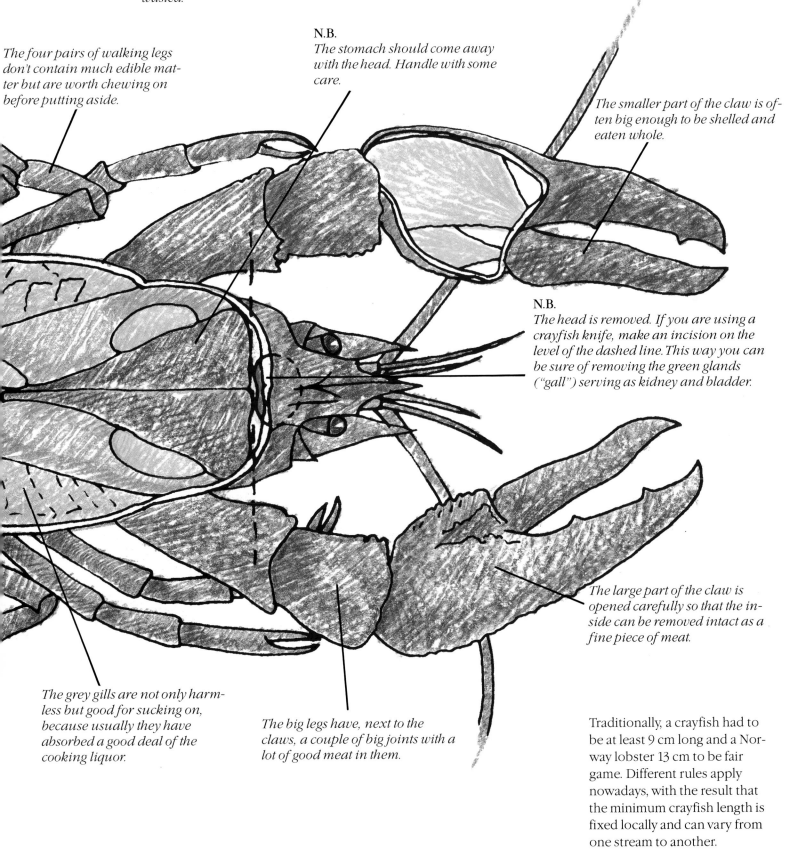

N.B.
The head is removed. If you are using a crayfish knife, make an incision on the level of the dashed line. This way you can be sure of removing the green glands ("gall") serving as kidney and bladder.

The large part of the claw is opened carefully so that the inside can be removed intact as a fine piece of meat.

The grey gills are not only harmless but good for sucking on, because usually they have absorbed a good deal of the cooking liquor.

The big legs have, next to the claws, a couple of big joints with a lot of good meat in them.

Traditionally, a crayfish had to be at least 9 cm long and a Norway lobster 13 cm to be fair game. Different rules apply nowadays, with the result that the minimum crayfish length is fixed locally and can vary from one stream to another.

Table sense and etiquette

There is relatively little meat in a crayfish and it is not all that easy to get at. You have to work for it!

This lack of volume can of course be made up for by numbers.

But there is also the question of technique – that is, getting as much goodness and enjoyment as possible out of every single crayfish.

No etiquette

There is no fixed etiquette for eating crayfish. If anything, the crayfish party is an occasion when we can let our hair down and not worry about other people seeing us.

A proper crayfish party is an audiovisual experience. The cooking liquor is there for slurping and the compacted goodness of a large, well-filled claw is also a feast for the eye and worth commenting on.

You can perfectly well put two or three crayfish on your plate at a time, but it is not good manners to ransack the pile for wide bottoms – females – or extra big claws. Let chance decide.

The use of fingers instead of conventional knives and forks also indicates a universally accepted, welcome relaxation of normal table manners.

This "bachelor's hall" ethos is underlined by the occurrence of large bibs, funny little hats and, not least, an unusually large number of schnapps drinking songs.

Crayfish are there to be enjoyed as well as eaten!

But a little sense

Since, though, there seems to be a certain amount of doubt concerning the fullest, simplest and safest way of enjoying crayfish and literally getting the most out of them, we've put together some illustrated hints on the next two pages.

Don't take the following description too seriously. Pick and choose for yourself among the hints we give, so as to develop a technique of your own. All we do promise is that if you follow our recommendations, what is left of the crayfish when you've finished with it won't be worth having.

Enjoying your crayfish

Begin by feasting your eye on the attractive presentation of the crayfish. Your taste buds will come to life, your expectations will rise. Time to get started!

1. Begin by stretching the crayfish to its full length and sucking at the fine liquor still inside and on it.

2. Now detach the two claws by holding the crayfish in one hand and with the other breaking the claw downwards against the body of the crayfish. This way the claws come off, joints and all.

3. Now you remove the only large part of the crayfish not to be eaten — the head. There are two schools about the best way of doing this.

3:1/1 Holding the crayfish firmly in one hand and the knife in the other, make an incision just behind the eyes.

3:1/2 Put the crayfish on your plate and cut right through it. Among other things you have now removed the (yucky) stomach, but presumably some of the "butter" — yellow in colour — remains. Scrape this out carefully with the knife.

When removing the head by this method, take care not to puncture the stomach, because that will just about ruin the "butter".

3:2/1 Holding the crayfish by the head and the upper part of the tail, carefully break off the entire head at the junction between body and tail.

3:2/2 Hold the head part with the back underneath. All the "butter" can now be carefully coaxed out. Be careful, so as not to puncture the stomach and ruin the "butter".

The advantage of this method is that you don't risk cutting through the stomach. The potential disadvantage is that you have to scrape out all the "butter" with the knife and may then puncture the stomach all the same.

The head and the big carapace go to decorate the rim of your plate, This way too, you can keep an eye on your score. But so, unfortunately, can the people next to you.

4. Now suck out the liquor from the region of the gills.

5. Now for the claw. The point of the stoutest part is broken off with the whole in the blade of a proper crayfish knife. Now you can remove the meat in one piece.

6. First, though, you have to make an incision along the edge of the claw and prise up the shell. The claw, we trust, will be packed with good meat.

7. The small part of the claw has no meat worth mentioning. But it is well worth sucking on.

8. The first intermediate joint of the claw is often stout enough to be worth scraping out.

9. Sometimes the claws may be so thick-shelled that dissection is difficult. A pair of crayfish tongs (or a nutcracker) will do the trick.

10. Now for the meaty tail. Grasping it firmly upside down, break (crack) the first two joints, with a knife if necessary.

11. Now the tail meat is partly exposed and you grasp it, at the same time giving the point of the tail a good pinch.

12. Pull out!

13. Split the tail part down the middle, so that you can remove the intestine. Lift the upper part clear, by folding it away from the lower part.

14. The intestine can now be picked off with your knife.

15. Now, either you have "lived from hand to mouth" or else you have laid up a store to be put on toast. Either way, it now only remains to chew carefully at the small but tasty legs. Chew and suck, but be careful not to swallow any shell!

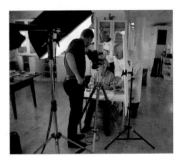

Björn Halling, culinary mentor

Björn Halling is one of Sweden's best-known cooks and, among other things, Principal of the Restaurant Academy in Stockholm.

As culinary mentor of this book, Björn has kept a watchful eye on everything we've had to say about food and, at times, drink as well. Not that he has interfered much with the delights presented by the other expert contributors. His main concern has been to pull the whole act together and guarantee its overall quality.

It was Björn, for example, who persuaded so many of his gifted colleagues to share their wisdom and spend time creating a large number of very personal recipes to go with our crayfish. He is himself impressed by the variety of the recipe section you will shortly be coming to.

Björn himself has been bold enough to present his own, traditional way of cooking crayfish, fully realising that there are "just as many best crayfish liquors as there are cooks". Recipes, hints and advice from this generous culinary expert of many parts will also be found under other chapter headings.

Björn Halling is a doyen of Swedish chefs. He started his career with Tore Wretman at Stallmästaregården, Stockholm, in the early 1950s, when he also studied for a year at Le Grand Véfour.

At the beginning of the 1960s Björn moved to Operakällaren, Stockholm, where he became Second Chef. He studied at Cornell University, USA, in 1969.

After a spell as Product Manager with the SARA group of restaurants, Björn opened and ran a restaurant – Gutekällaren – in Visby, on the island of Gotland, from 1973 to 1979. He then started off on his own at the Pelikan restaurant in Stockholm and since 1975 has been Principal of the Restaurant Academy, Stockholm.

For many years Björn was Chairman of the Swedish Executive Chefs' Association and President of the Nordic Executive Chefs' Federation. As a member of Sweden's national team in the 1964, 1968 and 1972 Frankfurt Food Olympics, he harvested a collection of medals which, in the normal run of things, Swedish Olympic entrants can only dream of.

Other distinctions include the gold medal and Findus fellowship of the Gastronomic Academy and the Cadier Spoon awarded by Lilla Sällskapet.

Björn Halling

A classical crayfish menu

The classical crayfish menu has a long history, going back to the days when Swedish crayfish were a good deal easier to come by, not least in terms of price.

But even when our own crayfish were fairly cheap food, they were served in a variety of ways. For some people, crayfish during the relatively short season – say four weeks at most – were the obvious starter, with toast and cheese, several times a week. In this kind of situation there was no question of lanterns or hats or any other festive accoutrements.

Improved communications and the development of refrigeration and transport technologies have made the world smaller and made it possible, once again, for anybody wishing to do so to eat crayfish both during the season and out of it.

Starter – crayfish
The really traditional crayfish menu opens with a mound of cold, boiled crayfish and the traditional accessories: white toast, crispbread, butter and cheese. On the subject of suitable cheeses, the reader is referred to the "Cheese" chapter on page 69.

Main course – wild duck
The main course is a roast wild duck, served in the old-fashioned way with a cream sauce made from the carcase and presented with lettuce hearts, sauté potatoes, blackcurrant jelly and sliced cucumber. The open season for mallard usually coincides more or less with the opening of the crayfish season, which gives us two *primeurs*.

Dessert – melon
The crayfish menu is rounded off with melon and raspberries. The orange-yellow Swedish netted melon is beginning to ripen and the last of the raspberries are still on the bushes during the more traditional crayfish season. Otherwise both blackberries and lingonberries are coming on nicely. I shall have more to say about handling and preparing your melon in the chapter "Desserts, cakes and pies" on page 140.

Old-fashioned roast wild duck

Ingredients to serve 6:
2 wild duck
1 kg potatoes
1 cucumber
salt
3 tbsp vinegar (Swedish *ättika*)
3 tbsp sugar
1.5 dl water
1/2 pinch white pepper
1-1.5 pinches salt
1 bunch of parsley

Sauce:
2 tbsp butter
1 shallot, sliced
1 sprig of thyme
1 bay leaf
1/2 tbsp white flour
3 dl double cream

Serve with: lettuce, blackcurrant jelly

Procedure:
1. Heat the oven to 225°. Truss the duck.

2. Slice the cucumber thinly, sprinkle with a little salt and compress between two plates.

3. Roast the duck for about 25 or 30 minutes.

4. Peel, quarter (or chip) and rinse the potatoes. Roast them in the oven.

5. De-bone the duck and keep them warm (60°).

Birth of a classic!

6. Melt the butter and brown the chipped-up carcass with shallot, thyme and bay leaf, sprinkle with flour. Dilute with 2 dl water, reduce by half, add the cream, cook for 6-7 minutes. Strain, add salt and pepper to taste.

7. Prepare a mixture of *ättika*, sugar, water, salt, pepper and chopped parsley.

8. Strain the cucumber before adding it to the mixture.

9. Carve and serve.

To drink? Robert recommends:
For classical wild duck I recommend a medium red wine without too much body, the emphasis being rather on refinement and maturity. For example, a Rioja (Reserva or Gran Reserva), a somewhat lighter St. Emilion of good medium quality, six or seven years old, or a Chianti Classico Riserva. Our only problem really is the pickled cucumber and the jelly, but we wash them down with mineral water – not wine!

Björn Halling

Old-fashioned crayfish bisque
with pike mousse

A hint from Björn:
Don't hesitate to make this soup with veal stock!

Ingredients to serve 4:
Soup:
20 live crayfish
butter
about 1/2 onion
about 1/3 carrot
a small piece of celery
some parsley sprigs
1 sprig of thyme
1/2 crushed bay leaf
freshly ground white pepper
2 tbsp tomato paste
2 tbsp cognac
2 tbsp sherry
2 dl white wine
1.5 l fish or veal stock
2 dl double cream
1 heaped tbsp white flour
salt, pepper
1 tbsp unsalted butter

Minced pike for the carapaces:
80 g fresh fillet of pike, de-boned
1 pinch of salt
white of 1 egg
1 dl double cream
a dash of Cayenne pepper

Procedure:
This is an old-fashioned, rather heavy classical recipe for crayfish bisque. Time was when there were plenty of busy hands in the kitchens, which explains how the mince to go with the carapaces could be prepared the hard way with pestle and mortar. The mortar was iced and the procedure both arduous and time-consuming. Today we use a food processor.

The bisque
1. Wash the crayfish carefully in cold water. Kill them by piercing with a kni-fe between the eyes. Remove the middle section of the tail shell and extract the intestine. This is vital, otherwise you get a bitter taste.

2. Fry the crayfish in butter until they are red all over. Add finely chopped onion, carrot and celery, herbs and tomato paste. Bring to the boil. Add the cognac, sherry, white wine and stock, heating thoroughly.

3. Add the cream and simmer under cover for eight or ten minutes. Remove the crayfish with a slotted spoon.

4. Extract all the meat from the crayfish. Discard the stomach, which is underneath the carapace. Reserve the carapaces and tails for garnishing.

5. Crush the rest of the shells in a mortar together with a little butter. Return the crushed shells and all scraps of meat to the soup and cook for another 10 or 12 minutes.

6. Strain the bisque through a fine strainer and then reduce. Thicken with 1 tbsp flour, kneaded together with soft butter.

7. Immediately before serving, add salt and freshly ground white pepper to taste. Add the unsalted butter for extra gloss.

The pike mince
1. Put the food processor jug, complete with knife, pike fillet and – in a separate vessel – the cream in the freezer for ten minutes, because it is vital for all the ingredients to be cold.

2. Begin by running the pike and salt at top speed, for a tough, hard mixture.

Don't forget the crayfish!

3. Add the egg white and process until the mixture is smooth supple and homogeneous; scrape down intermittently from the edges.

4. Add the cream in a fine jet, flavour with Cayenne pepper.

5. Transfer the mixture to a forcing bag and squirt it into the polished carapaces. Wedge a tail into each carapace and steam for 8 minutes on a low flame, i.e. below 100°, so that the mixture will coagulate without souffléing.

To drink? Robert recommends:
A generous, full-flavoured soup like this one, requires a drink with plenty of character. If we are going to have a dry white wine, it will have to be a full-bodied one with a touch of oak and maturity. Something superior, in other words. Things are a bit easier for the sherry fancier: try a small glass of dry Oloroso Viejo – guaranteed to provide an interesting gastronomic experience.

Portrait of Björn Halling on page 93.

Björn Halling

Crayfish salad from East Småland

A hint from Björn:
You don't have to be a native of Småland to appreciate this crayfish salad –
just three crayfish each can make life
easier for anybody!

Ingredients to serve 4:
12 large crayfish
0.5 dl crème fraiche
dill crowns
2 apples
about 1/2 cucumber
4 gherkins
balsamico vinegar
salt, pepper
4 medium-large tomatoes

Procedure:
1. Clean the crayfish.

2. Mix the meat from the joints and the
crayfish "butter" with the crème fraiche.

3. Pick the outermost flowers from a
crown of dill, chop finely and blend
with the crème fraiche.

4. Chop the (unpeeled) apples, the cucumber and the gherkins into small
cubes.

5. Blend the apple, cucumber and
gherkins with the crème fraiche, adding balsamico vinegar, salt and pepper to taste.

6. Divide and de-pip the tomatoes,
making long strips out of 3/4 and cutting 1/4 into a fan shape.

7. Take 4 low-sided dishes (about 10
cm in diameter). Line them with grease-proof paper, spread the salad on
this, invert on a plate (glass if possible)
and remove the paper.

8. Garnish with tails, carapace, claws,
tomato strips and dill.

To drink? Robert recommends:
This salad of Småland origin has ingredients which make the choice of wine
difficult. Instead one is put in mind of
a pale Swedish lager, well-hopped and
bitter. Similar beers from other countries, of course, will do just as well.

*Giant crayfish from Småland – slightly
counterfeit, but Oh! so good.*

Portrait of Björn Halling on page 93.

Nils-Emil's crayfish pâté with trout roe

A hint from Nils-Emil:
The 18th century Swedish troubadour Carl Michael Bellman and his lady-friend Ulla Winblad would have loved this one!

Ingredients to serve 4:
Crayfish pâté:
1 kg fillet of pike (fine-ground twice over)
1 tbsp salt
3/4 tsp white pepper
a *soupçon* of Cayenne pepper
a *soupçon* of fine-ground nutmeg
5-6 whites of eggs
1 l. double cream
500 g crayfish tails
2 dl fine-chopped dill

White egg dressing:
2 whites of eggs
4 dl cooking oil
2 dl crème fraiche
1 tsp Coleman's mustard powder
2 crushed cloves of garlic
salt, pepper
a few drops of Worchestershire sauce

Garnish:
Lettuce leaves, dill, 4 tsp trout roe

Procedure:
Crayfish pâté:
1. The mixture has to be cold. Blend it with salt, spices and egg whites.

2. Add the cream, a little at a time. Season to taste and carefully blend in the crayfish tails, (properly drained) and the dill.

3. Spoon the mixture into a greased pâté mould and cover over with foil. If possible, leave the pâté to stand for a day before cooking it.

4. Cook the pâté in a *bain-Marie* for about an hour and a quarter, in an oven preheated to 100°. Make a couple of small holes in the folio for the steam to escape through. Leave to cool.

The egg dressing
1. Whisk the egg whites lightly. Blend the oil, first a drop at a time and then in a fine jet, just as for mayonnaise.

2. Add the remaining ingredients and season to taste.

Serving:
Prepare medium-thick slices of the pâté. Lay them on plates and garnish with lettuce and sprigs of dill. Put the egg dressing to one side of the slices, topping with a teaspoon of trout roe.

To drink? Robert recommends:
Fish and shellfish pâtés make splendid starters and usually present no problem as regards the choice of wine. In view of the dill and trout roe, I would rather recommend a somewhat younger white, dry and fruity, fresh wine like Muscadet sur Lie or a Sauvignon Blanc. As always with roe or caviar, a dry champagne goes even better!

Ulla Winbladh would surely have loved this recipe, and it is served at the restaurant named after her.

Nils-Emil Ahlin
Today perhaps better known as Nils-Emil than by his surname, as a result of his two restaurants (Nils-Emil and Nils-Emils Bakficka) in Stockholm.

It all began in Hedemora, and Nils-Emil received his first restaurant training at the Hasselbacken Restaurant School. He then worked as a cook at the Cecil restaurant and, six years later, be-came head waiter at Stockholm's famous Operakällaren. France, England and Switzerland gave him more international experience, and he also studied for a while at Cornell University in the USA. Nils-Emil took part in the 1967 Montreal exhibition before returning to manage the Riche and Teatergrillen restaurants in Stockholm.

Nils-Emil founded Källaren Diana in Stockholm Old Town, which he ran until starting his two present businesses in 1985. It was in 1992 that Nils-Emil took over the Ulla Winbladh restaurant, which he still also runs. Nils-Emil holds the gold medal of the Gastronomical Academy, the Silver Spoon of Lilla Sällskapet and the title of Purveyor to the Royal Household (more specifically to H.R.H. Prince Bertil).

Jan Boris-Möller

On the morrow

A hint from Jan:
Don't mind if the party's over, because it never really is – count your leftovers and look to the future!

Ingredients to serve 4:
16 crayfish carapaces
1.5 l. crayfish liquor

Mixture
200 g fillet of salmon
1 egg (if the salmon was frozen)
3 dl double cream (milk, as a slimmer option, will do fine)
1 bunch of dill
salt and pepper

Sauce
all the claws that were left over and some of the crayfish shells
4 tbsp butter
1 carrot
1 onion
2 tbsp tomato paste
1 pinch of Cayenne pepper
1 tbsp flour
4 dl white wine
4 dl water
3 dl double cream
salt, pepper
Armagnac (optional)

Serve with: parboiled spinach

Procedure:
The mixture:
1. Run the fillet of salmon for 1 minute in a food processor. Add the egg and process for 15 seconds. Add 3 dl cream in a fine jet with the processor running.

2. Fold in the sprigs of dill and season with salt and white pepper. Leave to stand in a bowl for about an hour.

The sauce:
1. Put the claws and a little of the shells

in a saucepan. Add the butter and break up the claws and shells in it, using a beer bottle or some such object.

2. Peel and chop the vegetables. Mix them with the shells. Heat the crushed shells on the cooker, stirring occasionally.

3. Add the tomato paste, Cayenne pepper and flour. Mix all the ingredients thoroughly before adding the wine and water. Boil slowly for 10 minutes.

4. Add the cream and cook for another ten minutes.

5. Drain off the shells and vegetables. Season with salt and pepper and lace with a little Armagnac (optional). Keep the sauce warm.

6. Get out the mixture and spoon it into the carapaces.

7. Bring the crayfish liquor to the boil before putting the stuffed carapaces into it. As soon as it comes to the boil again, remove the saucepan from the heat and leave the carapaces for three minutes.

8. Remove the carapaces with a slotted spoon and place them on a little kitchen tissue.

9. Pour the sauce onto warm plates and position four carapaces on it. Serve with a little parboiled spinach.

To drink? Robert recommends:
In spite of its name, this is an elegant starter for a carefully worked out menu on a special occasion. A dry champagne makes a superb introduction to a festive menu and, with Jan's crayfish composition, is a gastronomical triumph. Serve a dry, tasty champagne, e.g. from Louis Roederer, Pommery, Bollinger or one of the other, similar houses.

"The morning after" – much better than it sounds, and we don't mean the cook!

Jan Boris-Möller
Unlike most of his colleagues, Jan is entirely self-taught, although his family circle brought him into early contact with the stately home cooks of Skåne. Their rather uniform style of cooking, though, rather encouraged him to find his own ways of doing things.

The art of cookery, for him, is something of a challenge, as any number of television viewers can testify.

After gathering first-hand experience of New York catering in the eighties, he now runs a complex business called "No problem" – the name says a good deal about him personally. Big parties

or small ones – it's all the same to Jan: he can provide both the food and the other arrangements. If, into the bargain, you would like som gentle instruction in the art of preparing good food, you needn't ask twice. And there will be plenty of laughter thrown in!

Karin Chädström

Crayfish cocktails

A hint from Karin:
A posh start and a painless one!

Crayfish cocktail with celery

Ingredients to serve 4:
iceberg lettuce
celery
dill
28-32 shelled crayfish tails

Vinaigrette sauce:
2 tsp white wine vinegar
a little crayfish stock
4 tbsp oil
a few crowns of dill, crumbled
salt, white pepper

Garnish: crayfish claws, dill crowns

Procedure:
1. Cut the iceberg lettuce and celery into strips. Mix with finely chopped dill and put into four cocktail glasses.

2. Now put 7-8 shelled crayfish tails in each glass.

3. Mix the vinaigrette sauce and season to taste. Scatter the sauce over the crayfish.

4. Garnish with claws and dill crowns.

Crayfish and papaya cocktail

Ingredients to serve 4:
lettuce
2 papayas
24-32 shelled crayfish tails

Vinaigrette sauce:
2 tbsp olive oil
2 tbsp balsamico vinegar
salt, white pepper

Garnish: lettuce leaves, dill

Procedure:
1. Strip the lettuce and divide between four cocktail glasses.

2. Peel and dice the papayas. Cut up the crayfish tails.

3. Mix the oil and vinegar for the sauce and season to taste.

4. Mix the diced papaya and crayfish tails with the vinaigrette sauce and scoop the mixture into the glasses.

5. Garnish with a little lettuce and finely chopped dill.

A cocktail makes a promising start.

To drink? Robert recommends:
Two variants of a classic starter mean many different drinks to choose from. White wine can be dry or medium dry, but whichever you prefer, go for a somewhat lighter wine with a fresh, fruity taste and without any oaky tang. Pale beers (lager or pilsner) can also go well, depending on what the main course is going to be.

Karin Chädström
A keen pioneer in the professional kitchen, she can be said to have followed in her mother's footsteps. For it was Karin's mother, cooking for families in the Växjö region, who laid the foundations of her daughter's development, mainly as a cold-buffet manageress. In the restaurant trade, Karin won her spurs at Tylösand and Falsterbohus.

Moving eventually to Stockholm, she worked at Berns, Riche and Källaren Diana. Tore Wretman was her mentor for many years, and for the greater part of the 1960s Karin was cold-buffet manageress at Operakällaren.

Karin has taught at the Restaurant Academy and has harvested a variety of distinctions, not least by virtue of her pioneering achievement. Thus she holds

the Diploma of the Gastronomic Academy for outstanding culinary achievements and became the first woman to receive the Sandahl Foundation's Honourary Diploma, partly in recognition of her achievements "as cold-buffet manageress for the development of gastronomy".

Karin is much in demand today as a columnist and jury member.

Anders Dahlbom

Browned crayfish tails with curry sauce, potato and tomato puré and apple pellets

A hint from Anders:
A recipe is for guidance and inspiration – not slavish obedience.

Ingredients to serve 4:
20 shelled Norway lobster tails
salt, pepper
about 150 g butter
2 Granny Smith apples
1 onion
1/2 tbsp curry
1 dl fish stock
1 dl white wine
4 dl double cream
4 medium-large potatoes
3 tomatoes

Garnish:
4 claws (in their shells), fresh herbs

Procedure:
1. Salt and pepper the tails and fry them a fine yellowish brown on both sides in 50 g butter. Put to one side and keep warm.

2. Use a de-corer or suchlike to extract 20 neat pellets from the apples. Save what is left for the sauce. Chop the onion fine.

3. Heat the remains of the apples with the onion and curry in 50 g butter. Add the stock and wine and cook for about another five minutes or until all the liquid has been reduced.

4. Add the cream and cook for about 4 minutes to thicken. Season and strain.

5. Bring the apple pellets to the boil in buttered (25 g) water put to one side.

6. Peel and cut up the potatoes.

7. Scald and peel the tomatoes. Cut up two tomatoes and dice a third.

8. Boil the potatoes with the two tomatoes until the potatoes are perfectly soft.

9. Strain the potatoes through a fine sieve, season and fold in the diced tomato and 25 g butter. Keep warm. (To present the puré really smartly, scoop into individual moulds and turn out onto the plate when serving.

Inspiring!

Serving:
Put the sauce in the middle of each plate, with the tails and apple pellets round it. Position the puré right in the middle, garnishing with a claw and an attractive herb.

To drink? Robert recommends:
Here we have a balanced symphony of aromas with overtones of mild curry and apple. An aromatic dish which, together with a dry, white, spicy wine made from the Gewürtztraminer grape, preferably a few years ago, can turn into a genuine culinary experience. Harmonisation of food and wine is one way of creating good taste experiences.

Anders Dahlbom
After and in spite of a successful school career in Halmstad, Anders felt like doing something more practical, and two years later he graduated, as first in his year, from the restaurant school in Halmstad. Next came three years at the good old Johanna restaurant in Göte-

borg, with a break for military service, and since then Anders has cut new teeth and laurels in the eminent kitchens of Grand Hotel in Marstrand and La Scala and Park Avenue in Göteborg.

In 1993 Anders was awarded the Cook of the Year Gold Medal of the Gastronomic Academy, and a year before

that he had collected what is known as the Goldfish.

Anders is a member of the Swedish team which, in Frankfurt in 1996, will be defending the Swedish cuisine against the toughest imaginable competition.

Thomas Drejing

A stew of crayfish and light-salted perch

A hint from Thomas:
Recipes are meant to give you ideas – not orders!

Ingredients to serve 4:
Vegetable stock:
3 dl celeriac, parsnip, leek and onion, peeled and chopped into centimetre cubes
2 tomatoes, quartered
2 cloves of garlic
tarragon stalks
2 dl dry white wine
5 dl water
5 pepper corns

Stew:
600 g perch fillet
salt for seasoning and salting the perch
500 g French beans
400 g small "almond" potatoes
16 signal or noble crayfish, live
3 dl vegetable stock
50 g butter, unsalted
1 sprig of tarragon

Procedure:
Vegetable stock:
1. Bring the vegetables, garlic, tarragon, wine, water and pepper corns to the boil.

2. Cook on a low flame for about 30 minutes.

Crayfish stew
1. Carefully rub salt into the perch fillets about 2 hours before the stew is to be served. Leave in a cold place.

2. Shell the French beans. Boil the potatoes, unpeeled, in salted water. Peel when ready.

3. Bring the vegetable stock to the boil again, put in the crayfish, bring back to the boil, put to one side and leave for five minutes.

4. Retrieve the crayfish, strain the stock. Save four whole crayfish, shell the rest.

5. Reduce the stock to a strong flavour (about 3-4 dl), season with salt (remembering that the fish is lightly salted already).

Stop here if you are preparing the stew in advance. Remember to cool the prepared ingredients as you go.

6. To finish off, bring the stock to boil in the pot you intend putting on the table. Add knobs of butter, followed by the potatoes and beans. On top of this, place the dried perch fillets, the shelled crayfish, the whole crayfish and the tarragon leaves.

7. Bring to the boil, remove from heat and leave to stand with the lid on until the perch fillets are ready (the meat must flake when pressed gently). Instead of tarragon you can use some other herb, such as crown dill, dill, basil or suchlike.

To drink? Robert recommends:
One good choice to this stew is a crisp, fruity Sauvignon Blanc with its distinctive character of unripe gooseberries and nettles. Though our Swedish friends in the Nordic archipelago would probably prefer a glass of fresh, pale lager, which is just as good a choice. But different!

A fine stew served with white farm bread. But... did Thomas pinch the fourth crayfish?

Thomas Drejing
In spite of his family having a restaurant tradition and although he himself started early, Thomas' choice of career was not automatic. In the end, though, the environment and genetics prevailed and he went to restaurant school in Malmö. After training he returned to his father's house in Växjö. But in 1979 Malmö summoned him again. This time it was the Primeur restaurant, where Thomas remained until 1981.

Thomas helped to start the Saison restaurant in Copenhagen's historic Österport district. Then in 1983-84 he worked in France, with the Troisgros brothers in Roanne and with Bernhard Loisseau in the Côte D'or.

Then it was back to Copenhagen, but before long he started up on his own and, since the autumn of 1984, has been running Petri Pumpa in Lund.

Thomas believes in combining high-quality "everyday raw materials" with a few other ingredients, without any frills and furbelows. Simplicity can sometimes be the difficult part.

Karin Fransson

Aubergine galette with crayfish and saffron sauce à la Provençale

A hint from Karin:
Crayfish with a touch of the south of France – spicy!

Ingredients to serve 4:
Sauce:
48 crayfish
3 shallots
1 large carrot
1 piece of celeriac
1 fennel bulb
1 piece of leek
3 tomatoes
4 cloves of garlic
olive oil
1 tbsp tomato paste
1.5 sachets of saffron
3 tbsp cognac
2 dl white wine
5 dl fish stock
1 sprig of tarragon
2 sprigs of thyme
1 pinch of Cayenne pepper
4 dl double cream
2 dl crème fraiche
salt, pepper
about 50 g butter
about 2 tbsp whipped cream

Vegetable mixture:
2 aubergines
salt
1/2 zucchini
3 tomatoes
3 spring onions
olive oil
2 cloves of garlic
3 tbsp chopped herbs, e.g. basil, parsley, dill, chervel and tarragon or 1/2 tbsp dried herbes de Provence and one tbsp chopped parsley and dill
salt, pepper
crayfish tails
white flour
lemon juice

Garnish: fresh herbs, black olives

Hot spiced crayfish – rosé!

Procedure:
The sauce
1. Begin by shelling the crayfish, removing the stomach at the front end of the carapaces. Also remove the intestine running the length of the tail. Save the tails and break the shell into pieces.

2. Clean, peel and chop the vegetables. Dice the tomatoes. Crush the garlic unpeeled.

3. Heat a little olive oil in a large pan. Brown the crayfish shells, followed by the vegetables, spoon in the tomato paste, scatter one sachet of saffron and fry for another few minutes.

4. Pour on the cognac and ignite or reduce. Pour on the wine and fish stock, add the spices and simmer until the liquid has been reduced by half.

5. Add the cream and crème fraiche and cook until the liquid has been reduced by another third.

6. Strain and squeeze out all liquid in the shells and vegetables. Bring the sauce to the boil again, seasoning perhaps with more saffron, Cayenne pepper, salt and pepper.

7. Transfer the whole thing to a food processor, adding about 50 g butter in small knobs. Return to the pot and add a little whipped cream just before serving.

The vegetable mixture

1. Slice the aubergines (lengthwise), salt them lightly and lay them on a plate turned upside down. Leave to drain for about two hours.

2. Slice and dice the zucchini into approximately 1/2 cm cubes, but remove the seeds.

3. Scald and peel the tomatoes, remove the pips and cut the flesh into the same size cubes as the zucchini. Draining the cubes a little is a good idea.

4. Slice the spring onion thinly.

5. Heat (but do not brown) a little oil in the pan and heat the zucchini and onion in it.

6. Crush and spread the garlic, scatter the chopped herbs, season with salt and pepper and, lastly, add the diced tomato and the crayfish tails. Swirl round and allow to warm only.

7. Get out the aubergine slices, wipe them dry with kitchen tissue, turn them in white flour and brown them well in olive oil.

N.B. Don't use too much olive oil: the aubergines are like blotting paper, even if the pan seems a bit on the dry side.

8. Put one slice on the plate, add a little of the crayfish mixture, cover with the other slice and spoon the sauce all round. Garnish if you like with fresh herbs and black olives.

P.S. Brushing the top of the aubergine with a little basil mixture is a tasty touch: mix a few basil leaves with a little olive oil, lemon juice, garlic, salt and pepper until you get a green oil.

To drink? Robert recommends:

Scents and flavours of Provence are the essence of this composition, so why not choose a wine to match? A Provençale rosé! Pale, rose-red with a young, fresh fragrance of grapes and a light, dry, fresh flavour with just a hint of grapy sweetness. But of course, other rosé wines of the same kind from other countries will also do well.

Karin Fransson
Karin came to Hotell Borgholm some years ago from Germany and was quickly snatched up by the then restaurant manager, Mr Fransson — for life!

Before long Karin's range of interests expanded to include the hotel restaurant, for which she developed a combi-
nation of Swedish home fare and traditional German cooking.

A research trip to France opened her eyes to the spices of the southern French cuisine, and her well-known recipes today are distinguished by a firm balance of Swedish and foreign ideas.

A Sunday television programme
made Karin a national celebrity in Sweden, and distinctions on the shelf back home in Borgholm include both a diploma from the Gastronomic Academy, Lilla Sällskapet's Silver Spoon and the Silver Medal of the newspaper Svenska Dagbladet.

Stefan Holmström

Crayfish and chanterelles in aspic with dill-spiced avocado cream

A hint from Stefan:
A crayfish borne up by products of the season.

Ingredients to serve 8-10:

This recipe can be halved (to serve 4 or 5), but in that case the aspic is best made in individual moulds.

Aspic:
250 g fresh chanterelles (small)
a pinch or two of sea salt (or ordinary salt)
freshly ground white pepper
50 newly boiled (Signal Crayfish)
3 dl white wine
4 shallots
1 carrot
1 piece of celeriac
1 tbsp tomato paste
1 bunch of crown or ordinary dill
(about 10 stalks)
15 sheets of gelatine
whites of two eggs

Avocado cream:
2 avocados, well-ripened
5 crowns of dill
5 tbsp Gourmet kesella
3 tbsp double cream
1-2 pressed lemon
salt and freshly ground pepper

Garnish: tomato, dill crowns

Procedure:
Aspic
1. Start by seasoning the chanterelles and then heat them for 10 seconds in the microwave or for a minute or so in the frying pan, reserving any liquid.

2. Shell the crayfish and put them in, when cool, with the chanterelles.

3. Crush or chop the crayfish shells,

put them in a saucepan and add water and the white wine. The liquid must cover the shells properly. Bring to the boil and skim carefully.

4. Peel and chop the vegetables. Stir the vegetables, tomato paste and crown dill into the liquid and let the whole thing boil slowly for about an hour.

5. Season to taste. Strain the liquid and leave to cool.

6. Put the gelatine to soak.

7. Put the egg whites in a stainless saucepan (thoroughly cleaned), whisk them slightly and pour on not more than a litre of the cool stock. Stir in the gelatine.

8. Bring to the boil, stirring carefully.

9. Strain, preferably through a cloth, and leave to cool.

10. Add the crayfish and chanterelles, pour into a smart aspic mould and cool for at least five or six hours.

Avocado cream

1. Peel the avocados and remove the seed.

2. Cut off the outermost seeds from the dill crown and crush them gently in a mortar.

3. Run all the ingredients in a food processor. Season with salt and pepper, adding a few drops of water if you think the cream is too thick.

4. Leave to stand for an hour or so, so that the fine aroma of the dill can pervade the whole thing.

Serving:

Heat the aspic mould carefully under warm water for a second or so and then turn out the contents onto a thoroughly cleaned chopping board. Cut into appropriate slices, placing these on properly cooled plates. Serve the avocado cream on the plate or in a side bowl. Garnish with a little chopped tomato flesh and one or two fine crowns of dill, finishing off with a twist or so of the peppermill.

To drink? Robert recommends:
A light, delicately balanced starter which must not be shouted down by an over-assertive wine. A somewhat lighter, medium-dry, white Riesling with floral, peach-like and honey-like fragrances from Mosel-Saar-Ruwer is a good choice. If you prefer a drier sort

Stefan will not admit to any specialities, but isn't there something rather special about crayfish and chanterelles in aspic?!

of Riesling, try one from New Zealand, for example.

Stefan Holmström
A young man delivering bread from the bakery to the hotel kitchen found the customer's business more interesting than his employer's. That, putting it rather drastically, is how Stefan got into the catering business.

Eventually he entered restaurant school in Göteborg, followed by Stora Hotellet in Jönköping. There were many

other halts along the way as well, most of them the length and breadth of Sweden. Especially memorable and instructive, though, was a five-year spell as chef at the Johanna restaurant in Göteborg.

Stefan has perhaps travelled more than most of us. He went round the world on the Älvsnabben training ship, and he has paid several visits to Belgium, Italy and, not least, France. For

some years now he has been running an eponymous restaurant in Halmstad.

Twice runner-up in the Cook of the Year competition, Stefan has won the Sweden's best desserts competition. If one asks for a speciality, he protests that a good cook must be able to cook good food and do it properly, with any raw materials whatsoever, so long as they are good ones.

Kenneth Ingelsson

Brochette of crayfish and shallots with papaya salsa and ginger sauce

A hint from Kenneth:
Real strength often lies in capitulation –
enjoy your crayfish!

Ingredients to serve 4:
Brochette:
32 crayfish tails
1 bay leaf
1/2 tbsp thyme
10 white pepper corns
3 tbsp cooking oil
8 ready-cooked shallots
4 wooden skewers
salt

Papaya salsa:
1/2 cucumber
1 red paprika
1 yellow paprika
1 papaya
a piece of leek, about 20 cm
2 cloves of garlic, chopped fine
2 tbsp jalapeños, chopped fine
juice of 1/2 lemon
a few drops of olive oil
salt, pepper

Ginger sauce:
0.5 dl sugar
0.5 dl white wine vinegar
1 tsp red chili, chopped fine
2 tsp ginger, chopped fine
0.5 l. crayfish stock
(arrowroot)
salt, pepper

Procedure:
Papaya salsa
1. Split the cucumber lengthwise and scoop up the seeds with a spoon.

2. Dice the cucumber, paprikas, papaya flesh and leek. Mix everything together and season to taste with garlic, jalapeños, lemon juice, olive oil, salt and pepper. Leave to draw for a couple of hours if possible.

Ginger sauce
1. Candy the sugar (i.e. heat until it is golden brown) in a saucepan. Add vinegar, chili, ginger and crayfish stock. Reduce to about 3 dl liquid.

2. Thicken, if preferred, with arrowroot diluted with a little cold water. Season with salt and pepper.

The crayfish brochette
1. Run the bay leaf, thyme and white pepper corns in the food processor. When they are crushed fine, add the cooking oil for a few seconds.

2. Peel, top and tail the shallots. Split them into 16 halves and put two crayfish tails round each half.

3. Put four onion halves and crayfish onto each skewer. Turn the skewer in the cooking oil, sprinkle with a little salt and grill.

Go on – spoil yourself!

4. Serve on warm plates with the papaya salsa in the middle and the crayfish brochette on top. Heat the sauce and pour a little of it round the salsa.

To drink? Robert recommends:
Kenneth's ginger sauce makes it hard to imagine drinking a wine with this dish. The ginger and sweetness of the sauce and the hotness of the jalapeños in the salsa immediately put one in mind of a refreshing glass of pale, cool beer with a touch of bitterness. Why not a pale, mild beer from Mexico?

Kenneth Ingelsson
Good seldom comes of coercion, but the fact is that Kenneth's interest in cooking began with catering fatigue during military service. The next step came in the mid-1970s, when, as a ship's cook, Kenneth visited exotic countries like Australia and New Zealand.

After a few years Kenneth returned to Sweden and the Johanna restaurant in

Göteborg. He brought with him not only fresh knowledge but a taste for exotic fruits as a distinctive element of his cooking.

Also in Göteborg, Kenneth worked at Göstas, Belle Avenue and Restaurang Arkivgatan. Then in 1987 he moved south to the fleshpots of Skåne and the Johan P restaurant in Malmö.

Kenneth has also shouldered his re-

sponsibility for culinary culture as a member of the Skåneland Gastronomic Academy and as Chairman of the Skåne Association of Professional Cooks.

Kenneth has turned his knowledge into competitive success and – more and more, lately – printed productions. He has co-authored a book and produced innumerable newspaper articles.

Örjan Klein

Boiled crayfish in saffron broth

A hint from Örjan:
Lots of quality and few calories!

Ingredients to serve 4:
20-24 boiled crayfish
5 dl fish stock
50 g leek, sliced
50 g celery, sliced
50 g zucchini, sliced
1 small carrot, in strips
1 bunch of crown dill
0.5 g saffron
salt, pepper
100 g cherry tomatoes

Procedure:
1. Shell just the tail of the boiled crayfish and remove the intestine.

2. Bring the fish stock to the boil and add the leek, celery, zucchini and carrot. Cut up the dill very small and add it with the saffron. Season to taste.

Serving:
Put the crayfish and tomatoes in soup plates and pour the dill stock over them.

To drink? Robert recommends:
The stock, with its character of saffron and crown dill, demands a fruity, neutral wine – for example, a Tokay d'Alsace, or a somewhat lighter Italian Chardonnay with no suggestion of oak.

... and a touch of saffron turns boiled crayfish into something quite new!

Örjan Klein
Örjan was only seven when the spectacle of his grandmother's herb garden brought home to him that food is what you make it.

*His career started at Hasselbacken in Stockholm, followed by Berns Salonger and, later, Den Gyldene Freden. On the way Örjan also completed a more formal chef's training which put him in charge of the kitchen at the Maxim res-*taurant. *During this period Örjan also visited France and improved his game with Roger Vergé, George Blanche and Troisgros. In 1976 he took the opportunity of putting all other competitors – a despairing home team included – in their places in a cooking competition in Trondheim where the main emphasis was on fish. For a long time, together with Tore Wretman, Örjan spread the Swedish smörgåsbord worldwide, and* in 1983 he accompanied the King and Queen of Sweden on their tour of Brazil.

Örjan received the 1983 gold medal of the Gastronomic Academy, followed in 1992 by the Cook of the Year award and, the year after that, by Tore Wretman's Prize of Honour.

Örjan is one of the authors of the Academy's cookery book. Today Örjan works at well-known KB in Stockholm and teaches at the Restaurant Academy.

Gert Klötzke
Stewed crayfish tails with small potato pancakes and fennel sauce

A hint from Gert: Not quite as easy as winking, but just as much fun!

Ingredients to serve 4:
Pancakes
150 g peeled potato
50 g white flour
3 eggs
0.5 dl double cream
salt, pepper
butter

Crayfish stock
400 g crayfish shells, carefully cleaned
3 tbsp olive oil
3 cl cognac
250 g carrots
50 g celery
50 g leek
50 g shallots
2 tomatoes
2 cloves of garlic
water
1 bay leaf
1-2 blooms of crown dill
1 tbsp tomato paste

Crayfish sauce:
5 dl crayfish stock
2 dl double cream
salt

Fennel sauce:
100 g fennel
2 tsp oil
0.5 dl white wine
3 dl ordinary fish stock
5 g butter
1 cl Pernod
salt, pepper
1 tsp (barely) lemon juice

Cooked crayfish tails:
3 dl crayfish sauce
40 large crayfish tails

Garnish: crème fraiche, fennel haulm

Potato pancakes – poor man's fare come up in the world!

Procedure:
The pancakes
1. Boil the potatoes.

2. Blend the flour, egg yolks and cream into a smooth mixture. Rice the potatoes and add them to the mixture.

3. Whisk the egg whites, fold into the potato mixture and season with salt and pepper.

4. Fry the pancakes in a knob of butter, using a griddle. Allow two pancakes per person.

Crayfish stock
1. Heat the cleaned crayfish shell in the olive oil. Add and ignite the cognac.

2. Cut the cleaned vegetables into small pieces and heat them with the garlic in a little oil for about 5 minutes.

3. Mix the vegetables with the fried crayfish tails. Add enough cold water to cover.

4. Bring to the boil and skim, add bay leaf, crown dill and tomato paste and leave to cook for another 45 minutes or so, skimming carefully all the time. Strain.

Crayfish sauce
1. Reduce the crayfish stock by half, add the cream and reduce on a low flame.

2. Season with salt. You can thicken the sauce with 1 tsp butter and 1 tsp flour, kneaded together and whisked into the boiling sauce.

Fennel sauce
1. Clean the fennel and cut it in strips. Save the haulm.

2. Heat the fennel in oil, add the wine and allow it to blend.

3. Pour on the fish stock and cook the fennel until it is quite soft.

4. Run the fennel in a food processor together with butter, Pernod and most of the fennel haulm (save a little for garnish), season with salt, pepper and a little lemon juice.

Cooked crayfish tails
1. Bring the sauce to the boil and add the crayfish tails. Save four nice tails for garnish. Do not cook the sauce after this.

Serving:
Put a potato pancake on the plate, followed by the cooked crayfish tails and another pancake on top. Pour a little of the fennel sauce round the pancake. Garnish with 1 tbsp crème fraiche and a nice crayfish tail, plus a little of the fennel haulm.

To drink? Robert recommends:
A composite starter, full of fragrance and flavour and with delicate touches

Sometimes the recipe even includes cognac!

of crown dill and fennel. This calls for a really responsive wine. Go for a superior French Chardonnay with plenty of grape, dry and full-flavoured with a balanced touch of oak. Chablis or Côte de Beaune will do fine if you can run to it. Good, attractively priced alternatives are often available from Côte Chalonnaise.

Gert Klötzke
Having grown up at the Stöllet Restaurant in northern Värmland, where his father Heinz was chef, Gert had little difficulty in deciding on a career.

Restaurant school in Sandviken and work experience in Sundsvall were followed by a spell at the Berkeley in London. On Gert's return to Sweden,

military service awaited him, as a highly qualified field kitchen commander! After further studies in Switzerland, he joined his father's business.

A desire to go his own way took him in 1973 to Värdshuset Flottaren in Vansbro. During this period Gert was elected both Cook of the Year and Game Cook of the Year.

At the beginning of the nineties, Gert left Vansbro for Rådhuskällaren and the Banken restaurant in Falun. Today he works at Loka Brunn and Grythyttan, as well as being team manager to Sweden's national cooking team. As a cookery book writer, Gert has left his mark on a variety of fields: game, food for athletes and Swedish party food.

Erik Lallerstedt

A "pastry" of crayfish and veal sweetbreads

A hint from Erik:
(Taken from the Eriks Bakficka menu)
It's your duty to enjoy yourself.

Ingredients to serve 4:
Pastry:
100 g veal sweetbreads
salt, pepper
white flour
butter
1 large aubergine
olive oil
20-24 traditionally cooked crayfish
tails (shelled)

Sauce:
2 shallots
butter
about 1 dl crayfish stock
1 dl double cream
2-3 tbsp butter
1 tsp white wine vinegar
a pinch of sugar

Garnish: trout roe

Procedure:
The sweetbreads have to be parboiled.
Rinse and put in cold, salted water (1
tsp salt/litre water). When it starts to
bubble, remove the sweetbreads and
pour off the water. Now put the sweetbreads in boiling salt water and cook
for five or ten minutes.

The pastry
1. Slice the sweetbreads. Dredge them
in salt, pepper and flour.

2. Fry the slices in a little cooking fat
for about 3 minutes.

3. Cut the aubergine into 12 slices,
brush the slices with olive oil and grill
or fry them.

Sauce
1. Chop the onion fine and heat it in a
little butter (don't let it change colour).
Add the crayfish stock and bring to the
boil.

2. Add the cream and reduce slightly.
Stir in the butter with a whisk. Add a
dash of vinegar and finish off with a
pinch of sugar.

Serving:
Start with a slice of aubergine and then
top with sweetbreads, aubergine, crayfish tails and aubergine in that order.
Pour the sauce round and garnish with
the trout roe.

To drink? Robert recommends:
A dish in which the main ingredients
have plenty of scope together. As a
starter, I could imagine serving it with
a tasty, dry white wine or a pale lager.
For a main course I would serve it with

Chopped chives make a fine garnish.

a fresh, light red wine with a gentle flavour and a touch of soft fruit about it. A
red wine like this should be served at
about 16-17°.

Erik Lallerstedt
*He controls with a loving hand a small
group of restaurants, having Eriks in
the Old Town as its central point. And
also including Eriks Bakficka and Tivo-
li Bar.*

*The whole thing really started at the
Waldorf Astoria in New York. Then,
back in Sweden, it was Hasselbacken
and – the first restaurant of his own –
Gerdas Fisk.*

*Stockholm's first floating restaurant
was Erik's idea, gaining Sweden's first
star in the Guide Michelin. It was back
to sea: again in the summer of 1993,
when he and Leif Mannerström worked
the west coast of Sweden, serving their
guests with good food and schnapps
drinking songs.*

*Together with Bengt Wedholm he took
part in the Stockholm Water Festival
where, as he puts it, they had "the*

*ugliest tent but supplied any amount of
good food and laughter".*

*Erik's many radio and TV appearan-
ces have made him one of the best-
known personalities of Swedish cuisine. He is widely consulted by hotels
and restaurants and many young
cooks will proudly tell you that they
have "worked for Erik".*

Eric Lips

Crayfish mousseline on leaves of spinach

A hint from Eric:
Cooking is a long-term art!

Ingredients to serve 4:
Crayfish stock:
1 kg boiled crayfish
2 tbsp oil
1/2 onion, chopped fine
1 piece finely chopped leek, celeriac, carrot
1/4 clove of garlic, chopped fine
1 tbsp tomato paste
1 pinch of sugar
cognac, white wine, Madeira as preferred
a pinch of tarragon, thyme and curry respectively
1 l. fish stock, home-made or cube
1 dl veal stock

Crayfish mousseline:
500 g boneless salmon, minced
2 eggs
salt
Cayenne pepper
5 dl double cream
crayfish coulis to taste (heavily reduced crayfish stock)
the crayfish tails

Sauce:
crayfish coulis
6 dl double cream
salt, pepper
Madeira, cognac
1 tbsp unsalted butter

Serve with:
Leaf spinach, finely chopped onion, salt, pepper, nutmeg

Procedure:
The crayfish stock
1. Shell the crayfish, remove the intestine and reserve the tails.

2. Dry the shells in the oven, then crush and mash them.

3. Heat the oil in a large saucepan, add the vegetables, the tomato paste and the sugar after a few minutes and heat together on a low flame for about 10 minutes.

4. Pour on and ignite the cognac, add the spices, the fish and veal stock, the white wine and the Madeira, then cook slowly for about 10 minutes.

5. Strain and reduce to about 1 dl. Cool.

The crayfish mousseline
1. Divide the minced salmon in half. Put

A work of art!

it in the food processor together with 1 egg, a little salt and Cayenne pepper.

2. Process briefly, adding 2.5 dl of the cold cream and a little of the coulis (small quantities at a time) until the consistency is right.

3. Put away in a cool place and then repeat for the second batch.

4. Strain.

5. Butter some coffee cups, put one crayfish tail at the bottom of each cup, split the remainder and fold them into the mixture.

6. Scoop the mixture into the cups.

7. Bake them in a circotherm oven on full vapour for 10 minutes at 100°. Or in an ordinary oven, using a bain-Marie, for about 20 minutes at 150°.

Sauce
1. Bring the rest of the crayfish coulis to the boil with about 6 dl of double cream, adding salt and pepper, Madeira and cognac to taste.

2. Reduce to the right consistency and finish off by stirring in 1 tbsp unsalted butter.

Serving:
Heat a little leaf spinach and finely chopped onion, season with salt and pepper and a soupçon of grated nutmeg. Transfer to warm plates, put the mousseline on top, cover with the sauce and serve.

To drink? Robert recommends:
The intrinsic taste of crayfish and salmon is reinforced by a very strong-flavoured coulis and by the inclusion of Madeira and cognac in the source, and so the wine must have plenty of cha-

racter. Choose one of the older, tasty dry whites, with a touch of oak, from Burgundy or Pessac-Leognan in the Graves region. Wines of the same sort from other regions will also do, of course.

...crayfish, salmon, cognac and Madeira – what do you drink with that?

Eric Lips
With his father, executive chef Hans Lips, as babysitter, Eric had his nose into the saucepans by the age of three and his future was decided. After winning his spurs in Switzerland and elsewhere, he came to Stockholm's historic Grand Hotel. The end of the 70s found Eric working abroad again, this time in France.

His next stop was Operakällaren in Stockholm, but then in 1984 he made for Skåne and the well-known Årstiderna in Malmö. Eric has kept faith with Skåne and, following touch-downs at the classic Savoy and Kramer, he is now executive chef at Trolleholm Castle.

As one might expect, Eric belongs to the Skåne Association of Professional Cooks. He enjoys working from heavy

old recipes, adding a lighter touch and a new garnish.

The surroundings of Trolleholm are conducive to a seasonal, traditional menu philosophy and both crayfish, eel, goose, game and Christmas fare are duly celebrated, the main ingredients coming from the castle's own hunting grounds.

Leif Mannerström

Crayfish with ginger dressing and chives

A hint from Leif:
Use the freshest crayfish imaginable.

Ingredients to serve 4:
16 large Norway lobsters, boiled
1 bunch of chives

Dressing:
1 tbsp fresh, grated ginger
2 tbsp white wine vinegar
1 dl oil
salt, pepper

Garnish: chive flowers (optional)

Serve with: toast

Procedure:
1. Split the crayfish, remove the intestine and stomach. Break the claws and arrange 8 crayfish halves on each plate.

2. Mix all the ingredients for the dressing, add salt and pepper to taste.

3. Pour the dressing over the crayfish and snip the chives over that.

4. Garnish with chive flowers and serve cold with toast.

Caught at sea and just landed!

To drink? Robert recommends:
A good, exciting dressing elevates a simple dish to big sensations of taste. A somewhat darker, top-fermented beer, like an English Pale Ale or a German Altbier, will go well. Gueuze Lambic, the spontaneously fermented Belgian beer, with its fruity, vinous style, merges well with the tone of ginger and is well worth trying.

Leif Mannerström
After instructive visits to both Europe and the USA, Transatlantic liners included, Leif returned to the west coast of Sweden and Göteborg as chef at Henriksberg in the beginning of the 1960s.

In the 1970s he earned top marks in Sweden for restaurang Johanna, before going off to Spain. In 1985 he returned to Sweden, to take charge of the SAS school of catering and cookery, he delighted the citizens of Malmö for a time

with a restaurant of his own, O'Yes, and today he is chef de cuisine at Park Avenue in Göteborg, his favourite city.

In the journal Restaurang & Storhushållsnytt in 1993, colleagues and rivals voted him best cook in Sweden.

Rickard Nilsson

Crayfish and basil omelette with ceps

A hint from Rickard:
An omelette with a character of its own!

Ingredients to serve 4:
Crown artichoke mixture
8 large, fresh Norway lobsters
2 crown artichokes
1 beefsteak tomato
4 large ceps or eight small ones
1 bunch of chives
butter
cooking oil

Crayfish sauce:
4 dl good crayfish stock
1 dl dry white wine
2 finely chopped shallots
3 dl double cream
salt, pepper and a pinch of sugar

Basil omelette:
1/2 dl water
1 bunch of fresh basil
2 eggs
salt and fresh-ground white pepper

Crayfish mince:
70 g salmon
4 crayfish tails
about 1/2 egg white
1.5 dl double cream
salt, pepper and a pinch of sugar

Procedure:
Crown artichoke mixture
1. Preheat the oven to 120°. Shell the Norway lobsters, reserving the shells for the sauce.

2. Cut out the hearts of the crown artichokes, divest them of coarse leaves and boil them in salted water. Leave to cool. Remove the "beard".

3. Cut each heart into small "cake slices", do the same with the tomato flesh and divide the ceps.

Crayfish sauce
1. Make a good stock from the crayfish shells. Now take 4 dl of the stock, add the wine and onion and reduce by half.

2. Add the cream and reduce to a thickish consistency.

3. Season with salt, fresh-ground white pepper and a pinch of sugar. Keep warm.

In Sweden you don't say cheese...

Omelette
1. Mix the water and basil, whisk in the eggs with a fork and season to taste.

2. Cook four thin omelettes in a lightly buttered teflon pan on a medium flame. Transfer onto grease-proof paper and leave to cool.

Crayfish mixture
1. Cut up the salmon and crayfish tails.

2. Run the salmon, crayfish tails and egg white in a food processor till thoroughly minced and mixed, and thin out with the cream.

3. Season to taste with salt, freshground white pepper and a pinch of sugar.

Final preparations:
1. Spread a layer of the mixture on the omelettes and roll up. Now wrap them in plastic film (like a sausage).

2. Put the "sausages" on a baking sheet with a little water on the bottom, and bake for about 20 minutes. Keep warm.

3. Heat the crown artichokes, the ceps, the tomato and a little finely chopped chives in a little butter. Season with salt and pepper.

4. Grill the Norway lobsters in a little oil, one minute per side.

5. Slice the omelette.

6. Dole out the sauce and omelette on the plates. Put artichoke mixture on each plate, topping with the Norway lobsters. Serve the remaining sauce separately.

To drink? Robert recommends:
Choosing a wine to go with an omelette is not always easy, and very often other drinks are preferable. The main rule is to go by the filling, if any. This time we

...you say omelette!

would like to serve a wine if possible, and we can: a dry white, preferably fairly neutral, full-bodied and with a discreet, mild taste. A Pinot Blanc from Alsace is often a good choice.

Rickard Nilsson
In his childhood home, Rickard soon learned that food has to be both shopped and prepared with care. Perhaps this is why he opted for catering studies in high school.

In 1986, after a couple of years "de-villing" locally, Rickard had the chance of working in what at that time was perhaps the most interesting restaurant in Sweden – Johanna in Göteborg.

Returning in 1988 to his native Skåne, Richard became first chef at Restaurang Fiskargatan in Lund. In 1991 he was nominated Cook of the Year and awarded the "Dairy Medal" of the Gastronomic Academy.

Today Rickard freelances, and is widely known to television audiences.

Claes Riddarström

Blanquette, Swedish style with chicken and crayfish

A hint from Claes:
Let cooking *and eating* take time!

Ingredients to serve 4:
1 chicken, weighing about 1.5 kg
20-30 crayfish
100 g dill
lemon juice

Stock:
the chicken carcass
1 l. water
1 carrot
1 onion
1/2 celery
dill stalks
thyme, bay leaf, white pepper
1 dl dry white wine
2 dl double cream
1 dl crème fraiche
butter and flour
horseradish

Garnish: small onions, button mushrooms, Swedish turnips, black radish, potato or mange-tout (vegetables according to season).

Procedure:
1. Draw the chicken and cut into 8-12 pieces.

2. Make stock from the carcass, water, vegetables and spices. Skim carefully all the time. Simmer for 1.5 hours.

3. Shell the crayfish.

4. Take half the chicken stock and the white wine and reduce to 2 dl. Add the cream and cook for another 5 minutes.

5. Add the crème fraiche and thicken with beurre manié (equal parts of butter and flour). Strain the sauce and season to taste.

6. Clean the vegetables for accessories. Chop the dill.

7. Rub the pieces of chicken with a little lemon juice and poach them in the remaining stock.

8. Meanwhile, cook the garnish vegetables in salt water with a little butter. Start with the hardest ones, adding the others as you go. If you're using potatoes, boil these separately.

Now – take your time!

9. Bring the sauce to the boil and, after adding the crayfish tails, heat carefully. Add grated horseradish to taste.

10. Drain the chicken carefully, place it on a warm dish together with the vegetables and pour the crayfish sauce over it. Sprinkle with the chopped dill.

To drink? Robert recommends:
This aromatic dish with its thick, gentle sauce, demands a wine with personality, preferably one with a balanced residual sweetness. Choose a Kabinett or Spätlese German Riesling from Rheingau or Nahe. These often have a good, peach-like fruitiness, with a suggestion of honey, and a wonderful balance between fruit, acid and sweet after-taste.

Claes Riddarström
Born in Stockholm but reared in Örebro, where a keen interest in cooking was part of the family scene, Claes came out top of his class at the Kristineberg catering school in Stockholm.
Since then he has gathered experience from Swedish and international temples of the culinary art, such as Öhrns Hörn, La Brochette, L'Amandier de Mougins and Eriks Fisk. Today he works at Stockholm's famous Den Gyldene Freden.
Claes has often made the experts sit up and take notice, and he has been nominated for a number of Swedish culinary distinctions.
Claes is readily inspired by the classical French, Italian and Swedish cuisines and has found a style in which the food remains true to its origins.

Severin Sjöstedt
A crayfish salad for August with crayfish and chervil

A hint from Severin:
Salad – a splendid variation of crayfish!

Ingredients to serve 4:
120 g mixed lettuce
1 kg boiled crayfish, about 24
2 dl crème fraiche
2 tbsp Dijon mustard
crayfish liquor to taste
1 big bunch of chervil
fresh-ground white pepper
1 lemon
1 farm loaf
olive oil for frying, about 2 tbsp
150 g Chèvre (goat's milk cheese)
3 tbsp nut oil

Garnish: chervil

Procedure:
1. Rinse the lettuce and drain well.

2. Break the tails off the crayfish, shell them and remove the intenstine. Cut off the claws and remove the flesh carefully.

3. Mix crème fraiche and mustard in a bowl, scoop in the crayfish butter and stir. Dilute with a couple of table spoons of the crayfish liquor to taste (adding a little water if the sauce turns out too thick), chop and add half the chervil and then add pepper and a little lemon juice to taste.

4. Slice the bread, divide into strips (3 per person) and fry them in the olive oil.

5. Preheat the grill.

6. Spread the goat's milk cheese on the strips of bread and place on a baking sheet.

7. Pour the nut oil into a mixing bowl and toss the lettuce in it carefully.

8. Fluff the lettuce in the middle of each plate, group the claws round it and the tails in the middle, and then trail the sauce round the outside.

9. Heat the strips of bread in the oven until the cheese melts, put three on each plate and garnish with chervil.

Salad – but for gourmets, not slimmers!

To drink? Robert recommends:
A splendid salad with several dominant features. Melted goat's milk cheese on farm bread fried in olive oil, plus aniseed aromas from the chervil in the sauce and garnish. The classic accompaniment to goat's milk cheese is dry white wines from the upper Loire valley – Pouilly-Fumé and Sancerre, for example – or else go for a Sauvignon Blanc of similar character. The cheese and bread are also a good reason for trying a light or medium-bodied, fruity and young, rather robust red wine.

Severin Sjöstedt
Severin is the third generation of restaurateurs in his family.

He cut his own teeth at the Maxim restaurant in Stockholm during the mid-1970s. This was followed by Paris and the Copenhague restaurant, from which he returned as sous-chef at Stockholm's well-known KB (Konstnärsbaren).

The ensuing period comprised more work in France, at La Poularde, and in Copenhagen with Erwin Lauterbach at the Saison restaurant. Severin then joined a project team to transform the world-wide catering activities of the IKEA furniture company, a brief which included masterminding IKEA's restaurant management training.

In 1990 he opened his own restaurant, Tures, in Stockholm, while doubling as an adviser and product developer in the food industry.

In October 1993 he opened Severin Restaurant Naturhistoriska Riksmuseet.

Bengt Wedholm

Freshwater crayfish and pike mousse in Sauterne sauce

A hint from Bengt:
A French classic which I love making.

Ingredients to serve 4:
1.5 kg live crayfish
water, salt

Sauce:
1 onion
2 medium-sized carrots
crayfish shells
50 g butter
1/3 bottle of Sauternes
4 dl double cream

Pike mince:
300 g fillet of pike
salt
2 eggs
about 3 dl double cream
pepper

Procedure:
1. Rinse the crayfish carefully in running water. Bring about 4 l. water and 2.5 tbsp salt to the boil. Boil the crayfish for about 9 minutes, transfer to a colander and leave to cool. Reserve the water.

2. Break off the tails and shell them. Save the shells and the rest of the crayfish.

Sauce
1. Chop the onion and carrots finely. Crush the crayfish shells.

2. Melt the butter in a saucepan and heat the vegetables in it for a couple of minutes. Add the crayfish shells and cook for a few minutes. Pour on the wine and crayfish water so as to cover the shells. Cook slowly for about 15 minutes.

3. Strain the stock and reduce to about half. Pour in the cream and continue cooking until you get a thick sauce. Add the crayfish tails but do not allow to boil.

Pike mince
1. Put the fillet of pike through the mincer. Transfer to a food processor and place, with the other ingredients, in the refrigerator for about 1 hour. Everything *must* be cold.

2. Salt the mince and process at full speed for about 1/2 minute, add the eggs and then the cream, a little at a time

Bienvenu! To Sweden.

until you get the right consistency. Add salt and pepper to taste.

3. Butter four timbale moulds, scoop in the mixture and cook in a bain-Marie at 150° for about 30 minutes. Cover with grease-proof paper after the first few minutes.

Serving:
Turn out onto plates. Spread the crayfish sauce over and round.

To drink? Robert recommends:
A creamy sauce incorporating Sauternes points us in the direction of Bordeaux, more exactly Graves. Serve a dry white, medium bodied wine with a balanced oak flavour and of as high a quality as you think fit.

Bengt Wedholm
A veteran among Sweden's master cooks, he started from the bottom and knows the restaurant business inside out, from the vantage point of both kitchen and waiting staff.

His track record, beginning with Den Gyldene Freden in Stockholm, includes

most of Sweden's classical restaurants.

A stint at Cecil in Stockholm was followed by six years in Paris, and then for example by Trädgårdsföreningen in Göteborg, Snäckgärdsbaden in Visby, Strand in Båstad, Operakällaren and Rosenbad in Stockholm, Falsterbohus and, also in Stockholm, a longish stint

at Östergök until, in 1969, Bengt closed the circle by returning to Den Gyldene Freden.

There he stayed until 1982, when he opened his own, specialised Wedholms Fisk restaurant, which remains a delight to himself and to innumerable lovers of good food.

Birgitta Sidh

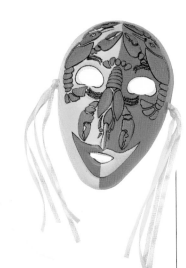

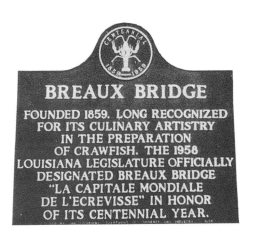

The American tradition

The Swedes are sometimes tempted to believe that theirs is the only country on earth where people eat crayfish, so deeply rooted is the tradition. Wrong!

In southern Louisiana, with its enormous wetlands, crayfish exist and are caught and eaten in incredible quantities. Every self-respecting restaurant has its own speciality. New Orleans has always been famous for its exquisite cooking and Brennans, Antoines and the Commander's Palace all have the most fantastic crayfish creations to choose from. Unceasing creativity makes the Creole kitchen tremendously exciting and vibrant, and Cajun cooking is no less interesting.

"Long live the crayfish" became in 1958 the motto of the small Cajun town of Breaux Bridge near Bayou Teche, which that year was nominated La Capitale de l'Ecrevisse, i.e. world crayfish capital. Within a radius of about 50 miles, more crayfish are produced than anywhere else on earth. Some – granted, not completely reliable – sources put the annual output at no less than ten million tonnes.

Those living in the region regard the crayfish as "manna from on high": it is self-producing and easy to farm and catch.

In the picture opposite we have geared up for a real Crawfish Fiesta, and in the next column is Jonas Borssén's version of the unusual, steamy recipe. With warm crayfish, hot spices and music signed Dr John, we are more than halfway to Louisiana already!

Crawfish fiesta

Fed up with the traditional Swedish crayfish party? Fond of spicy food and hot rhythms from Louisiana? Then here's an alternative containing both recipe and music.

Ingredients to serve 4:
2 onions (halved)
2 carrots (cut in large pieces)
6 small potatoes (peeled)
2 corn cobs (cut in large pieces)
2 stalks of celery (cut in large pieces)
2 spicy sausages (cut in large pieces)
corn oil
4 cloves of garlic (chopped fine)
1 lemon (rinsed and halved)
1 tbsp Cayenne powder or 2 fresh red chilies (chopped large)
1 tbsp paprika powder
2 tbsp ground fennel seed
3 bay leaves
2 tbsp oregano
3 l. water
about 1.5 dl salt 1 kg live crayfish

Procedure:
1. Heat the vegetables and sausage in a little oil. Add the spices and continue cooking on a low flame.

2. Pour in the water and salt, bring to the boil and season to taste; perhaps you will want to adjust the salt or seasoning. Cook for another minute or so.

3. Put in the crayfish and continue cooking, with the lid on, for about 6 or 7 minutes.

4. The green vegetables must be soft when everything is retrieved and transferred to a table covered with newspaper. Eat the crayfish warm and serve with lots of beer.

Crawfish fiesta music
The music flowing from the loudspeakers is signed Dr John, Clifton Chenier, and next in line are the Neville Brothers and Professor Longhair or perhaps Texas Tornados and Willy de Ville. *Laissez les bons temps rouler!*
Jonas Borssén

To drink? Robert recommends:
These crayfish have a hot rhythm of their very own. To match the spicy character and origin of this dish, we have put out a couple of thoroughly refrigerated bottles of slightly bitter, pale American beer.

Birgitta Sidh

Crawfish Cardinale

A hint from Birgitta:
The original recipe comes from Antoines in New Orleans.

Ingredients to serve 4:
20-24 large crayfish tails/crayfish
1 tbsp crayfish butter (if possible)
2 tbsp butter
4 tbsp onion or shallot, chopped fine
2 tbsp white flour
2 dl single cream
2 tbsp tomato paste (not ketchup)
2 tbsp cognac
4 tbsp white wine
1 pinch of Cayenne pepper
2 pinches of paprika powder
salt, white pepper
1 pinch of grated nutmeg

Procedure:

1. Shell the crayfish and reserve the tails. Crush the shells if you like, and put them in a saucepan with a little butter. Pour on just enough water to cover the shell. Bring to the boil and then simmer for about 40 minutes.

2. Strain the mixture while it is boiling hot. Discard the shells. Leave the stock to cool until the butter comes to the surface, forming a thin crust. Use the butter. The stock can be used for diluting with or for making a fine crayfish soup.

3. Heat the crayfish butter together with ordinary butter in a thick-bottom-ed saucepan. Add the onion and heat until golden yellow and soft.

4. Sprinkle the flour and stir well. Add a little of the stock (if you boiled the shells) and the cream. Cook for a few minutes, stirring all the time.

5. Add the tomato paste, the cognac and the white wine. Season well with Cayenne pepper, paprika powder, salt, white pepper and a little grated nutmeg. Lastly, add the shelled crayfish tails and heat – but do not boil – the mixture.

6. Serve in small bouchés or vol-au-vents or with boiled rice. The mixture can also be served in a crisp pie crust or simply with toast.

To drink? Robert recommends:
A dish full of flavour and fragrance and with nicely hot seasoning, and so the white wine served with it will have to be pretty full-bodied but not too dry or fresh. We want it to have plenty of fruit taste, with fairly rounded acidity. Go for a New World Chardonnay, not one of the greatest and most refined but a tasty, well-made wine of medium quality. By all means a wine with the *kiss of oak*, which can add an extra dimension to the interaction with aromas from the cognac and nutmeg.

Birgitta Sidh
A combination of circumstances and fatherly advice put Birgitta on the way to becoming a domestic science teacher, a profession which she has practised in the Stockholm Vocational Schools and at the Hasselbacken Restaurant School. Her ambitions grew and a two-year spell in the USA led to a Master of Science degree.

Returning to Sweden she took charge of a newly started experimental kitchen for the agricultural sector, where she remained for 16 years. But America beckoned again, this time to the post of cookery editor-manager with an international publishing house.

Birgitta was for several years Chairman of Lilla Sällskapet and has co-authored numerous cookery books in Sweden as well. She holds an award (1972) from the Gastronomic Academy and is now a freelance editor and columnist.

Jonas Borssén

Crawfish Gumbo

A hint from Jonas: Spice is life!

Ingredients to serve 4-6:
Gumbo:
1 packet of bacon (in strips)
200 g Cabanossa sausage (thinly sliced)
4 onions (chopped fine)
1 large yellow paprika (diced)
1 large red paprika (diced)
5-6 celery stalks (chopped fine)
2-3 cloves of garlic (chopped fine)
1 tbsp chili powder
1 can of crushed tomatoes
3/4 dl rice
1 l. crayfish stock
2-3 bay leaves
2-3 tsp oregano
1-2 tsp thyme
fresh-ground black pepper and sambal oelek to taste
100 g ochre (sliced)
about 2 dl white flour
400 g shelled crayfish tails or about 1 kg whole crayfish with the tails shelled but not detached.

Potato salad:
4 medium size potatoes (boiled, peeled and cut in pieces)
6 hard-boiled eggs (chopped fine)
6 spring onions (cut thin)
1 celery stalk (finely diced)
1 small red paprika (finely diced)
2 tbsp French mustard
1 dl mayonnaise

1 dl sour cream
salt and fresh-ground black pepper

Procedure:
Crawfish Gumbo

1. Heat the bacon and sausage in a big pan.

2. Add the vegetables except for the ochre and spice with chili powder. Stir carefully all the time, so that nothing sticks or takes on too much colour.

3. Add the tomatoes, rice and stock and reduce the heat. Simmer gently for about an hour, skimming off the fat as you go and transferring it to a cast iron saucepan.

4. After all the fat has been skimmed off, add the spices and ochre to the soup.

5. Heat the fat in the saucepan and stir in the flour. Stir or whisk carefully until the flour has browned. N.B. Be very careful about this, because it sticks easily. This is called making a "roux", and it will give the soup a distinctive character.

6. Stir the roux, a lump at a time, into the soup and whisk it to a suitable soup consistency, allowing the soup to come to the boil.

7. Season to taste: perhaps you would

like to make it spicier. Add the crayfish, mixing the tails and whole crayfish to make a good showing.

Potato salad
Mix all the ingredients in a large bowl. Season with salt and pepper. Serve cold.

Serve the gumbo with a dob of potato salad.

To drink? Robert recommends:
This dish is characterised by a lot of flavour from many ingredients with strong personalities. Sambal oelek, Cabanossa sausage and chili powder give it just the right hotness. The drinks with which it is served have to be thirst-quenching, so in addition to the mineral water we put out a dry white wine with a light, young, rather neutral and fresh taste. If beer is preferred, I would recommend a pale lager or pilsner.

Jonas Borssén
A cook who has certainly "got that swing". Not least when given free reign to his love and knowledge of the hot music and cooking of the American Deep South. The above recipe was dedicated to President Bill Clinton when he took office.

Behind him Jonas has a solid, traditional training which started at restaurant school in Göteborg (1977-79).

That was followed by no less than 8 years at Victor's Hotel and Restaurant. In 1986, to get more scope for his own ideas, Jonas started a freelance business, Amigo del Chile, which made him private chef to Bruce Springsteen & E Street Band in Stockholm and Copenhagen, lecturer, recipe developer, television and radio broadcaster and a contributor to magazines and cookery books.

Between 1987 and 1991, though, he

was permanently linked to the O'Yes Bar and Restaurant, in partnership with Victor Waldenström. Trade journals voted O'Yes Restaurant of the Year in 1987.

Jonas has had experience of working in both France and the USA: in 1986 at La Bonne Auberge on the French Riviera, and in 1993 as sous-chef with Christer Larsson at the newly opened and highly successful Christer's in New York.

Björn Halling

Desserts, cakes and pies

Both the classical crayfish menu and the traditional crayfish party often end with a melon-based dessert. Things can be made even simpler by serving ice cream, which is easily varied. Sometimes, though, one likes to spring a surprise on people, and so here is a slightly different recipe, using a puff pastry. If the dessert has not been too massive, a gateau or pie always goes down well with the coffee. With this I have used the classical soft fruit – raspberries, currants, blueberries and lingonberries – because they are so closely attuned to the crayfish.

Melon

As the picture shows, different kinds of melon can be used: netted melon, watermelon with its beautiful red flesh, or aromatic green Galia melons, variously served. One smart but also delicate way of serving small melons is with red port in the seed cavity. Melon and red port are the best of friends, providing a conclusion as pure as it is simple.

To drink? Robert recommends:
From left to right
Raspberries in Galia melon: an aromatic Galia melon filled with tasty raspberries go perfectly with a medium-sweet wine, such as a Coteaux-de-Lyon from the Loire.
Slice of melon with raspberries: Ruby port goes very well with this simple, tasty dessert, and so does a sweet Sauternes of superior quality.
Half a melon filled with port: classically simple and good. Accompanied by a glass of the same kind of port.
Half a melon filled with melon balls, raspberries and blackberries: several different nuances of flavour are met together in this half-melon, and full justice can be done to them by the somewhat neutral background of a sweet, white port.
Melon with strawberries, raspberries, blackberries and red currants: a cascade of colours and flavour impressions which really freshens up both palate and mind. Serve this splendid mixture with a sweet, aromatic Muscat, and remember to serve the wine at 10° or 12°.
Melon balls in melon: the Charente department of France is known, not only for its cognac but also for its good melons. A classical dessert, as good as it is simple. Fill the cavity with melon balls, top up with Pinot de Charentes and have a glass of the same.

Vanilla ice cream with red currants
Fresh and simple, the heading speaks for itself. By all means garnish with peppermint or lemon balm.

To drink? Robert recommends:
If the ice cream dominates, you should go for a sweet fortified wine. The sweetness and chill of the ice cream demand a response from the wine which few, if any table wines are capable of providing. Here, the ice cream being served with red currants, we can go for a sweet young Muscat. If, instead of the red currants, we serve the vanilla ice cream in a nut pastry case, we can substitute a sweet sherry or the Italian Vin Santo.

Puff pastry crescent with ice-cold double cream and raspberries

Ingredients
1 packet of puff pastry
castor sugar
2 dl double cream
0.5 l. raspberries

Procedure:
Cut large crescents (15-18 cm) of ready-made, rolled puff pastry, sieve castor sugar over them until they are white all over and bake at 200° until the sugar has turned golden brown and all the pastry is pale brown inside. It mustn't be white, because then it would taste stodgy. Cut up while hot, adding ice-cold double cream and a small coffee cup of raspberries. Serve immediately, because the temperature contrast is part of the experience.

To drink? Robert recommends:
Delicious! Bring out the acid aroma of the raspberries with a young ruby port or a sweet fruit or berry wine. We can also augment the burned aromas and the fragrance of the raspberries with the honey sweetness of a Sauternes or Sauternes-like wine.

Raspberry or currant cake

Ingredients:
Sponges:
3 eggs
2 dl sugar
2 dl white flour
2 tsp baking powder
1 dl warm water
1 tbsp butter
1 tbsp brown dried bread crumbs

Vanilla cream:
2.5 dl full-cream milk
1 egg
2 tbsp flour
2 tbsp sugar
1 vanilla pod split down the middle (1 tsp vanilla sugar will do)

Garnish: 1 l. raspberries/currants, cream

Icing for the currant cake: Egg white, juice of 1/2 lemon, castor sugar

Procedure:
1. Beat the egg and sugar fluffy.

2. Mix the white flour and baking powder and fold into the mixture. Add the water.

3. Grease and breadcrumb a cake tin. Spoon in the mixture and bake at 175-200° for 30-40 minutes. Leave to cool and then divide into three rounds.

Vanilla cream
Mix the ingredients in a stainless saucepan, heat thoroughly, whisk vigorously, cool quickly.

Final preparations
Mix the cream with 1/3 whipped cream, spread on the first round and sprinkle with berries. Do the same with the second and cover with the nicest one.

Raspberry cake: finish off with a topping of whipped cream and raspberries. *Currant cake:* garnish with icing, made as follows. Mix egg white, lemon juice and enough castor sugar to stop it being too runny. Beat with the electric whisk for 8-10 minutes. Cover the cake with the icing, garnish with bunches of currants and sprinkle with castor sugar.

Lingon and Chinuski flan

Chinuski is an oriental kinsman of our ordinary caramel sauce, to round off the acidity of the lingonberries.

Ingredients:

Flan case:	Chinuski:
130 g butter	2 dl double cream
1 dl sugar	0.5 dl treacle
3 dl flour	1 tbsp cocoa powder
0.5 dl water	1.5 dl sugar
	50 g butter
	1 tsp vanilla sugar

Garnish: lingonberries

Procedure:
Flan case
1. Mix the butter thoroughly with the sugar and flour. Add the water and work rapidly into a dough. Squeeze out the dough in a wide pie mould, preferably with a detachable bottom, taking care to ensure that the dough projects about 1/2 cm above the edge.

2. Line the inside of an aluminium foil and, as ballast, fill with split peas or something else which won't mind a spell in the oven. Bake for 20 minutes at 200°.

Chinuski
1. Cook cream, treacle, cocoa and sugar for 12 minutes, stir in the butter and then the vanilla sugar.

2. Spread the Chinuski over the bott-

om of the case and fill up with the lingonberries. Leave to cool. Serve with custard or whipped cream.

Blueberry pie

Ingredients:
Pie case:
4.5 dl white flour
150 g butter
pinch of salt
3 egg yolks

Filling
3 egg whites
1 dl sugar
1 l. fresh blueberries

Procedure:
1. Preheat the oven to 200°.

2. Mix all the ingredients for the pie case, which will be firm and slightly crumbly. Press out the dough in a spring-clip cake tin 24 cm in diameter (2 litres), so as to cover the entire tin, sides included.

3. Beat the egg whites until stiff.

4. Mix the sugar with the blueberries, fold into the egg white.

5. Fill the tin with the mixture and bake for about 50 minutes.